Royal Horticultural Society

GROW YOUR OWN
CROPS IN POTS

Royal Horticultural Society

GROW YOUR OWN
CROPS IN POTS

WITH 30 STEP-BY-STEP PROJECTS USING VEGETABLES, FRUIT, AND HERBS

Kay Maguire

Special photography by Steven Wooster

MITCHELL BEAZLEY

To Jo, to Kip and Matilda and to Mum and Dad

RHS Grow Your Own Crops In Pots
Kay Maguire

First published in Great Britain in 2013 by Mitchell Beazley,
an imprint of Octopus Publishing Group Ltd, Endeavour
House, 189 Shaftesbury Avenue, London WC2H 8JY
www.octopusbooks.co.uk

An Hachette UK Company
www.hachette.co.uk

Published in association with the Royal Horticultural Society

ISBN 978 1 84533 686 8

A CIP record of this book is available from the British Library.

Packaged by Griffin Books
Commissioning Editor Helen Griffin
Publisher Alison Starling
Art Director Jonathan Christie
Senior Art Editor Juliette Norsworthy
Designer Lizzie Ballantyne
Copy-editor Joanna Chisholm
Senior Production Controller Lucy Carter
Proofreader Annelise Evans
Indexer Michèle Clarke
RHS Publisher Rae Spencer-Jones
RHS Editor Simon Maughan

Set in Frutiga and Glypha

Printed and bound in China

The Royal Horticultural Society is the UK's leading gardening
charity dedicated to advancing horticulture and promoting
good gardening. Its charitable work includes providing
expert advice and information, training the next generation
of gardeners, creating hands-on opportunities for children
to grow plants, and conducting research into plants, pests,
and environmental issues affecting gardeners. For more
information, visit: www.rhs.org.uk or call 0845 130 4646.

Contents

The fruit and flowers of a strawberry plant prove that container crops can be as attractive as they are tasty.

There's a home-grown revolution going on...

Try growing your own delicious food

Kay Maguire: 'Growing your own makes you happy, healthy, and it's fun too!.'

Over the last few years there has been a surge in the popularity of growing your own food, and it's estimated that a quarter of Britons now do so. In many instances this trend has been fuelled by concerns about climate change, rising food costs, 'air miles', and the simple desire for fresh, healthy, 'real' food.

It's probably no coincidence that this has occurred during a time of global economic crisis. Although growing some of your own food won't solve your financial worries, any gardener will tell you that gardening makes you happy and keeps you sane. Add to that the fun, sense of satisfaction, and utter joy that eating something you have grown yourself brings and it is no wonder so many people are giving it a go.

And I don't believe it's a passing phase. Apart from the fact that the growing-your-own movement has been driven by real need – whether financial, environmental, or a yearning for delicious food – it is also kept going by the interest of gardeners. Once you've dabbled in this hobby there's little inclination to retreat!

I began growing food in the late 1970s, with my Dad on an allotment; and 30 years later we are both still at it. There's just no comparison between the plastic-wrapped fruit and veg on the supermarket shelves and something you have grown from seed, tended, and nurtured against the worst of the weather and munching slugs. The food is fresh, healthy, often free from chemicals and guilt, and tastes amazing.

Pots of herbs and salad leaves are easy to look after and develop quickly, so are great first crops to get you started in growing your own food.

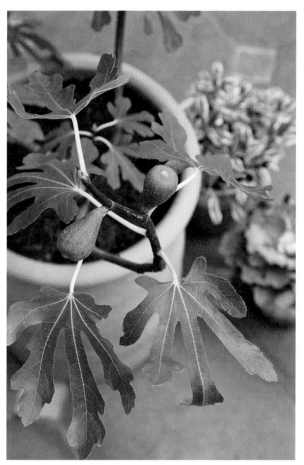

Figs grow almost better in pots than in open ground, because constriction around their roots encourages them to fruit well.

Growing crops in pots gives absolutely everyone the opportunity to have a go. The greatest uptake of grow your own has been in towns and cities, with urban gardeners grabbing what space they can. Urban areas generally enjoy sheltered microclimates – often sun traps – which are just perfect for growing fruit and vegetables.

Therefore anyone with a windowsill or access to the space on which to stand a few pots can grow a little food. It's the perfect solution if you have very little space, as you can use wall pots, windowboxes, and hanging baskets. Even if you have little or no earth, you can still grow food on a roof terrace, balcony, or patio. As you can see, you don't need an allotment or a large garden – in fact you don't need a garden at all.

Because pots have their own dedicated soil, it is possible to try crops you couldn't otherwise. For example, you can sow carrots in the fine-textured compost that they relish, and ignore any surrounding garden soil that may be very stony, or you can enjoy container-grown, lime-hating blueberries in a garden that may have chalky soil. In a pot you can also confine thuggish, invasive plants such as mint and horseradish, while nursing tender crops such as citrus or grapes, moving them to shelter in winter in cool-temperate areas. Pots are therefore the answer if your garden has difficult or tricky soil for example, if it is boggy or very dry and poor.

Container-grown plants can look great too, creating a striking feature on a patio or by a front

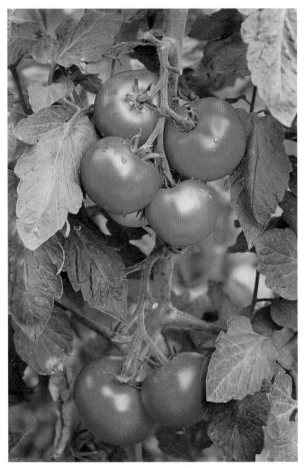

Tomatoes have long been a favourite crop for growing in pots, but these hungry, thirsty plants do need regular care.

Carrots grow really well in containers, where you can give them the perfect, stone-free soil they need.

door. The effect is enhanced when the crop looks particularly attractive. Beans, chard, and rhubarb, for example, all look wonderful, and lettuces come in a wide range of colours and textures. Edible crops can be mixed with containers of ornamentals to stunning effect. You can overcome the problems associated with monoculture, too, by encouraging a host of beneficial insects drawn by an array of enticing flowers.

RHS Grow Your Own Crops In Pots gives you everything you need to know about growing fruit, vegetables, herbs, and other edible plants in pots, from getting started to when to harvest. It includes pot sizes, feeding regimes, and compost types, and recommends varieties that fare best in a pot. You can then feel confident to have

a go, even if you have never grown an edible crop before. Fortunately most plants look after themselves provided they are fed and watered regularly. If things do go wrong, you will learn from it and get it right next time. By keeping container-grown plants close to the house, they will be quick to access and easy to care for.

Begin with your absolute favourite food, whether it is strawberries or peas, and then move on to something a little different next year, such as squash, borlotti beans, or pak choi. You will soon discover that growing edible crops is fun and very satisfactory – and might just change your life.

Crops that are grown simply for their edible leaves can create a stunning display, full of varied textures and visual interest, when combined in a carefully chosen container.

Techniques & Tools

Planning ahead for a successful harvest

Before you start, think carefully about what your crops need. Give them the best possible chance with the ideal spot – most require warmth, good light, and shelter. Keep container-grown plants well out of the wind, where they would dry out quickly. If you can, plant them up *in situ*. Pots full of compost, even small ones, are heavy.

Make sure your container is large enough for your crop, and remember that the smaller the pot the greater the demand for water and nutrients. Quick, shallow-rooting crops such as salads or strawberries can go in grow-bags and hanging baskets. Most crops require a pot at least 30cm (12in) in depth and width, and fruit trees and crops such as rhubarb and horseradish may need pots as big as 90cm (36in), if not bigger.

There are hundreds of lovely pots out there, in myriad designs, so consider their size, shape, weight, and material before you choose.

Terra cotta This is the traditional choice of pot. It looks great and is heavy and stable, which is handy for large, tall crops, although not if they need moving to warmer shelter over winter. Terra cotta is porous, so dries out quickly and is not

Terra-cotta pots look fantastic, but may need lining with bubble wrap to help in reducing the drying out of compost and to insulate plant roots in winter.

frost-proof unless it says so. Glazed terra cotta is slightly tougher than unglazed.

Plastic and fibreglass As well as being cheap, tough, and retaining water well, these materials are light and the pots comparatively movable.

Metal adds a modern touch or a retro look depending on type. It is tough, light (unless lead), and retains water well. Metal gets cold in winter and hot in summer and will eventually rust, so insulate and protect the insides with cardboard or bubble wrap before planting.

Wood is light and strong, but needs lining with plastic to stop it rotting.

Hanging baskets and windowboxes are great for making optimum use of vertical space and can contain a surprisingly large harvest.

Recycled containers Old sinks, baths, olive-oil tins, old boots, wine crates, buckets – the list of usable containers is endless. You can grow crops in just about anything as long as it is big enough and sturdy enough with adequate drainage holes. Drill some yourself if you need to.

Grow-bags These cheap alternatives to a pot are perfect for shallow-rooting crops.

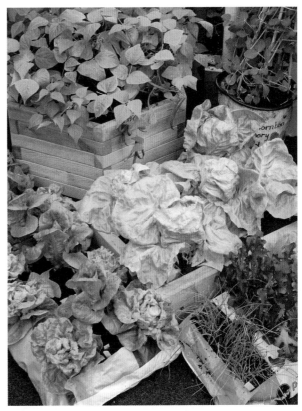

Different crops will thrive in all sorts of containers whether traditional wooden troughs, grow-bags, or recycled plastic tubs. Just ensure all containers have good drainage holes before planting.

Essential kit for crops in pots

- Pots
- Potting compost
- Drainage material
- Mulching material
- Hand trowel and handfork
- Watering can/hose and rose
- Secateurs
- Stakes, canes, twigs
- Twine
- Cloches, fleece, netting
- If you are busy, away a lot, or simply have lots of pots, invest in an automatic or drip irrigation system

Certain crops may benefit from additives to the growing medium. Perlite (centre) and vermiculite (right) will both help improve drainage for plants that need a lighter compost.

Always use fresh potting compost when sowing seed or potting up. Recycling old compost can be problematic because it often harbours disease.

When planting up pots it is a good idea to add slow-release fertilizer to the potting compost, to help plants once they have used up the original store of nutrients in the compost.

A mulch of gravel or pebbles will help to conserve moisture for this herb collection and will also keep water away from their crowns to prevent rotting.

Potting composts

The very best thing you can do for your crops in pots is provide them with good-quality potting compost. Multipurpose, soilless compost is a perfectly good growing medium for most crops, but it does vary in quality, so do not just go for the cheapest. Since it is light and free-draining, multipurpose compost dries out quickly and can be difficult to re-wet.

If you are growing tall crops or plants for longer than a season, use a loam-based compost, which is heavier and more stable than a soilless one and it also holds onto water and nutrients better. Specialist composts are also available, depending on your crop – look out for ericaceous compost for blueberries and specific citrus compost. And don't be tempted to use ordinary garden soil because it may contain pests and diseases.

You may need to add perlite or horticultural grit to the compost to improve drainage. Also mixing in food such as slow-release fertilizer granules, garden compost, or well-rotted organic matter, as well as rootgrow to aid root development, at planting will give your plants a good start. Water-retaining gel can stop pots drying out, but don't add so much the compost gets waterlogged.

Old pots are useful inside larger containers to reduce the amount of compost needed, making them lighter and cheaper to fill.

Fertilizers

If you did not add slow-release fertilizer when planting, any nutrients contained in potting compost will be exhausted after about six weeks. It is then up to you to feed your plants. You can topdress with dry fertilizer, or use a liquid one. A regular balanced feed will improve all your crops, but for maximum fruit you need one that is potash-rich. Chemical fertilizers such as liquid tomato food are available, but organic feeds, usually made from seaweed or comfrey, are also excellent all-rounders. Alternatively you can add comfrey leaves to compost at planting time or make your own liquid tea by soaking comfrey leaves in a bucket with water for a few weeks.

Drainage materials

Good drainage is absolutely vital in pots. Water must be able to flow away freely, so make sure you line the bottom of the pot with plenty of drainage material – crocks (broken pieces of terra-cotta pot), stones, gravel, and pieces of polystyrene packaging are all good. Cover the holes at the bottom of the pot with such drainage materials to stop them getting blocked by plant roots or soil. Raising pots up onto feet, bricks, or blocks of wood also improves drainage and is especially helpful if conditions are wet.

Mulches

Mulch is a key ingredient when growing in pots. It is, quite simply, a layer of anything that sits on the surface of the compost. It reduces moisture loss, acts as a barrier against weeds and pests, prevents compaction, and helps to insulate plant roots against cold weather. Mulch can also reflect or absorb light and heat depending on its colour. Look out for slate, pebbles, crushed shells, and glass beads. The best type of mulch feeds your crops at the same time. Bark, well-rotted organic matter, home-made compost, and leafmould all provide extra nutrients as they break down.

There is no doubt that edible crops can also look attractive. This sweet pepper easily holds its own with the black-eyed Susan (*Thunbergia alata*).

Choosing & buying suitable seeds or plants

Hundreds of crop varieties are specifically selected for container growing. Sometimes called patio varieties, they have been bred to be compact and bushy and include types of peppers, tomatoes, squash, peas, and beans; almost every fruit, vegetable, or herb has at least one container variety. They will certainly give you a good chance of success, but you do not have to grow only these.

Choose varieties that aren't too vigorous, and in cool-temperate areas look for varieties that crop quickly or early – this is important with vegetables such as tomatoes or aubergines that need a long growing season and would otherwise struggle in a short summer outdoors. When choosing fruit trees opt for those on dwarfing rootstocks or they simply won't survive in a pot.

Once you've chosen your varieties, always get the best-quality seed and plants you can. Now is not the point at which you try to cut costs. Organic seed and young plants are widely available, but consider growing heritage varieties too. Most of these have long histories of cultivation, and they are frequently more interesting and tastier than those on general offer. They are also open pollinated, which makes them ideal for seed-saving at the end of the year if you fancy having a go (see p31).

Catch crops & intercrops

All plants grow at different rates, which is good news if you want to make the most of the space in your pots and sow fast-growing crops in otherwise bare patches of soil. Sow intercrops at the same time as slower-growing crops such as beans, parsnips, or onions and harvest them while you wait. Alternatively sow catch crops in spaces that appear as you harvest other crops. You can sow whole rows or just dot in a few seeds as gaps pop up.

- Beetroot
- Carrots
- Chard
- Lettuce and salad leaves
- Radishes
- Spinach
- Spring onions

Radishes are perfect for growing with other crops. They are fast to harvest, ready as little as six weeks after sowing.

Most crops have at least one variety, and probably more, that will thrive in a container. Included here are purple-leaved basil, variegated oregano, and red-edged lettuce.

When investing in a fruit tree look for a nursery that holds local varieties. A tree that has been bred with your local environment in mind is likely to be happier, healthier, and more successful than any other. Otherwise visit a specialist nursery where you will get specific advice about container growing and the best rootstocks and types of tree.

What can't grow in pots

Sadly a small number of crops are definitely best left in the ground. Perennials such as Jerusalem and globe artichokes are simply too big and greedy for even the largest pots, while a crop such as asparagus, which takes years of patience to bring to harvest, would yield only the smallest of crops in a container, albeit a fine one.

Most brassicas need firm soil to keep them stable and to produce a decent heart, something difficult to achieve in a pot, and they are slow growing. If you have any open garden at all grow these beautiful plants there instead.

Always look for strong, healthy plants when buying fruit trees. They are an investment and will be with you for a long time.

How to establish all kinds of crops

If you don't have the time, space, or inclination to grow your crops from seed, or have simply missed the opportunity, young plants are readily available to buy as seedlings, plugs, or larger plants ready to plant out. Although fewer varieties are offered compared to seed, plants are usually ready from spring onwards. You will have more choice if you go to specialist nurseries rather than your local garden centre.

If buying tender vegetable plants such as beans and courgettes harden them off before they go out permanently, once the danger of all frosts has passed. Acclimatize them over the course of a week by putting your new plants outside during the day and bringing them indoors overnight so that they gradually get used to the change in temperature and general outdoor conditions. When you finally plant them out, do it in the morning if you can, so they have the whole day to settle in. Make sure you are ready to pot up your new purchases as soon as they arrive, otherwise keep them well watered until you can.

Planting up young plants

1 Water the plants while still in their pots.

2 Line the bottom of the pot with drainage material (see p15) and add potting compost (see p14) to just under the depth of your new plants. Mix in any grit that might be needed for drainage or slow-release fertilizer now.

3 Tease apart the plants' roots if there is more than one plant in the same pot, and plant individually, firming the compost in gently as you go. Leave 2cm (³/₄in) between the top of the compost and the pot rim to make watering easier.

4 Mulch with gravel or organic matter, and water the plants in well. Make sure slug and snail control measures are in place (see p32).

Seed sowing directly into pots outdoors

Most crops can be sown directly outside when the time is right, usually as the days get warmer in mid-spring, and this is easily the simplest, cheapest, and most time efficient way of growing most vegetables and many herbs.

1 Break up any lumps of compost with your hands or a hand rake.

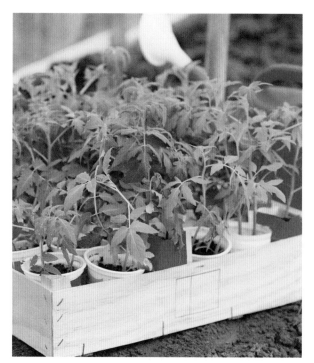

Tomatoes, whether sown by you or a nursery, will need growing on indoors before they are ready to go outside.

Most seedlings such as this spinach need thinning so that plants have room to grow well. Overcrowding can lead to weak, disease-prone plants.

2 Water the compost – this stops smaller seeds being washed around and helps germination.

3 Mark a drill, or make holes with a dibber.

4 Sow pinches of seed thinly in the drill. Drop larger, individual seeds into the holes.

5 Keep the compost moist while seed germinates.

6 Thin out seedlings to give them space to grow well. Thin to their final spacings when they are about 3cm (1¼in) high.

Starting seed indoors

Some crops such as tomatoes and aubergines need to be sown indoors if your climate does not have the long, warm summers such plants need to germinate, mature, flower, and fruit. By growing such plants from seed you can benefit from the large selection of seed varieties. You will also get a head-start with other more tender crops that cannot be sown outdoors until later in the season, such as beans, courgettes, pumpkins, and sweet corn.

Fortunately you don't need much equipment. A propagator is handy, although a warm, bright windowsill will do. Any small pot (with drainage holes) including old yogurt pots will work, or make your own from newspaper or recycled toilet roll tubes. Otherwise modular trays with individual cells are well worth investing in – one seed goes in each cell, so no thinning is required, and they are ideal for crops such as coriander and peas that hate root disturbance.

A warm, sunny windowsill is a good first home for many seedlings and young crops, provided that it is well lit.

1 Fill pots or a modular tray with potting compost and tap down so that it settles.

2 Water the compost with a fine rose.

3 Thinly scatter seed onto the surface of the compost or make a shallow hole and push individual seeds into each, following the instructions on the seed packet for sowing depth and germination conditions.

4 Cover the pot or tray with cling film or an inverted, clear plastic bag, and seal.

5 Place on a warm, light windowsill and keep the compost moist while seed germinates.

6 As soon as seedlings appear take off the cover.

7 When the first true leaves develop transfer the seedlings into larger individual pots. When doing this always handle the seedlings by their leaves rather than their stems, and plant each seedling up to its first true leaves.

8 Pot on again, a few weeks later, into larger pots.

9 When frosts have passed, harden off plants and then plant out into their final containers.

Planting a fruit tree

Make sure your pot is large enough – your tree will be in there a long time. Go for a pot a couple of sizes bigger than the one it came in; a pot 40cm (16in) in diameter is a good-sized first one, but remember in a couple of years the tree will need potting on into a bigger container. If you have a bare-root tree, make sure the roots have plenty of room to spread out.

1 Soak trees in water to give them a good drink before planting.

2 Line the bottom of the pot with drainage material (see p15). Add sufficient soil-based compost on which to sit the rootball and gauge the depth. You should be able to see the soil mark on the stem, showing at what depth the tree was previously planted.

3 Plant it at this depth, making sure there is a 3–4cm (1¼–1½in) gap between the surface of the potting compost and the rim of the pot.

This standard peach will need potting on into ever larger pots every few years as it grows, until it is in its final pot of about 60cm (24in) in diameter.

4 Fill in around the roots with compost, firming gently until the tree is sitting snugly in the pot.

5 If your tree needs staking, use a short stake – you only want to secure the roots against the wind, not to stop the whole tree from moving. Knock two thirds of the stake into the compost and tie it loosely to the tree.

6 Water in well and mulch.

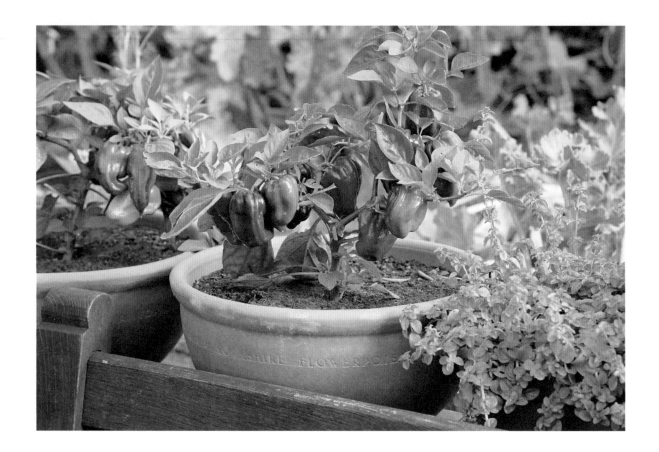

How to nurture & protect your crops

There is no getting around the fact that plants in pots need more attention than those in the ground. They are living off a limited supply of water and food and are reliant on you to keep that supply topped up. Do so and most of your crops should tick along quite happily, but occasionally plants need a little extra attention – some require pruning or tying in to supports, others may need protection against pests or moving to a sheltered spot.

Whatever the task is it won't be difficult – the beauty of growing in pots is that everything is small scale. Give your crops what they need, and it will make all the difference to the harvests you reap at the end of the season.

Be vigilant. During the summer growing months you need to check your pots every day, sometimes twice, but a quiet stroll in the mornings or with a glass of something in the evenings is a small and surprisingly pleasant price to pay to ensure your crops are in good shape. As well as ensuring you don't miss anything – be it wilting leaves, a munching caterpillar, or a crop that is ready for picking – such a routine will save you time and effort in the long run.

Watering

This will be your main occupation when growing plants in pots; you may as well face that fact right from the start. Never assume that recent rainfall will have done the job for you, especially if pots are sitting in rain shadows cast by a wall or fence. Make life easy for yourself by keeping pots close to a tap and by investing in a decent hose – ferrying watering cans backward and forward becomes anything but a labour of love after a while, no matter how small your area for containers. Get a spray gun with a rose pattern or a rose for your watering can to avoid compacting the soil surface. If you are planning on having lots of container-grown pots invest in a suitable irrigation system.

Feeding

Feeding is almost as important as watering, and different crops all have their own needs. Most plants require a regular feed during the growing and fruiting seasons. Once the nutrients in the compost run out – after about six weeks – it is up to you to provide the source of nutrients. One of the easiest ways to remember when to feed your crops is always to do it on the same day of the week. It should then slot neatly into your routine and hopefully you won't ever forget.

Ensuring crops are in good condition

It may seem a bother, but keeping your plants well tended increases yield and makes sure they are in good health. Herbs benefit from regular picking and pinching out of the growing tips to encourage lots of young, bushy growth, while edible flowers need constant deadheading to help more flowers to develop. Support tall plants such as beans, peas, cucumbers, grapes, and trained fruit trees with wigwams, obelisks, and canes, tying them in every now and then to guide them in the right direction. Give fruit trees and bushes at least an annual prune to keep them in shape, promote fruiting, protect them from disease, and extend their lives.

Watering your pots will be your main job in the summer months, with some crops such as tomatoes needing watering every day. Do this early in the day or in the evening.

Regular feeding is vital for strong, healthy, productive plants. Use ready-made fertilizer, diluted if appropriate at the recommended rate, or make your own comfrey tea (see p15).

Mint plants are always best grown on their own in pots rather than with other plants, which they can overwhelm.

Planning for holiday cover

Before you go away:

- Move plants to the shade, grouping pots together to help increase humidity.
- Place generous-sized saucers beneath all pots and fill them with water.
- Mulch plants if you haven't already, to prevent moisture loss.
- If you are away for only a few days make your own drip-feed bottle. Punch a small hole in the lid of a little water bottle filled with water. Turn it upside down and bury it cap-end in the compost. The water will slowly seep into the soil.
- Splash out and invest in an automatic watering system.
- Ask friends or family to check on plants while you are away.

Pollinating

A small number of crops benefit if you help them with pollination. Fruit trees such as peaches or plums may be in flower when few pollinators are about; in this case transfer the pollen from flower to flower with a small brush by rubbing gently

Above: Bees are most welcome pollinators, buzzing around flowers like this raspberry in spring and summer.

Left: Place pots together to create a mini microclimate. Plants will provide shade for each other, and humidity is increased.

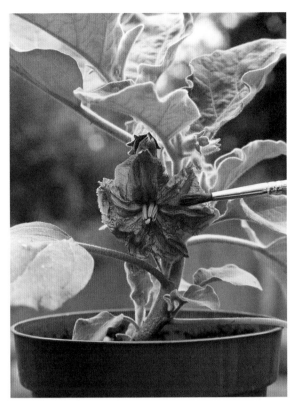

If insects are lacking in your garden or you are growing on a windy site, help plants such as aubergines by pollinating flowers gently with a small brush.

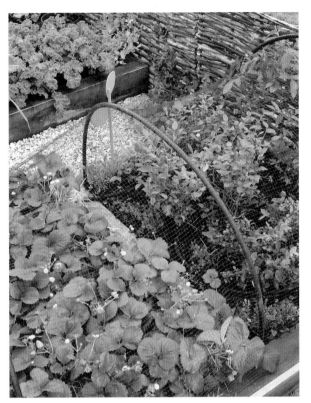

Protect fruiting plants such as strawberries from the birds with a diamond-mesh netting. Support it on hoops and stretch it tautly across plants so as not to trap birds.

on the stamens. Wind-pollinated sweet corn may need a swift tap to the tassels to help pollen dust the female flowers below. Pollination information can be found where appropriate in the individual directory entries, but some tips include:

aubergines – brush flowers (see p82);

chillies and sweet peppers – brush flowers carefully (see p83);

plums – rub blossom with a brush (see p53);

runner beans – mist flowers with water to help them set (see p118);

strawberries – rub flowers gently with a brush (see p70);

tomatoes – shake or mist flowers to transfer pollen (see p76).

Potting on

Every two or three years all perennial plants need transferring into larger pots filled with fresh compost. If possible give them the next pot size up, but once they reach the largest size – generally 50–60cm (20–24in) in diameter – just give their roots a prune before replanting them in fresh compost in their previous pot. In the years when potting on is not done give plants a boost by scraping away the top 5cm (2in) of soil and replacing it with fresh compost every spring.

Providing the optimum growing environment

Having raised strong, healthy plants it is important to nurture them in as helpful an environment as possible. That 5cm (2in) layer of mulch is a vital weapon in helping your plants grow strongly and healthily so they are more able to resist pests and diseases. It is also a good idea to erect barriers to protect your plants if you suspect problem pests such as birds, insects including caterpillars and beetles, or even hungry mice, are likely to attack (see pp32–35).

An industrial container such as this makes a great raised bed. It is wide and deep enough to grow a whole range of crops.

Above left: Ladybirds are invaluable in the garden and are one of our main helpers in the war against aphids.

Above right: A nest-box will help to attract birds to the area.

Encourage beneficial insects and natural predators into your garden by growing as diverse a range of plants as you can. Mix things up by placing pots of different crops next to each other and plant combinations of crops in larger pots. Growing herbs, flowers, and well-known companion plants with your fruit and veg will attract pollinators such as bees and helpful insects such as ladybirds, hoverflies, and lacewings (see box opposite). This is much easier to arrange if using pots than on a veg plot, where plants are often grown in rows and blocks of single crops. Think of your pots as a community of plants. Diversity will bring balance and if you can mix in some helpful, beneficial plants then all the better.

Having an area of water nearby, even a tiny one, can also bring in birds and insects, even frogs and toads if you are lucky. A bird bath would help, but a large, glazed pot, filled with water and a couple of aquatic plants, could attract some surprisingly helpful visitors to help tackle any pests.

Companion plants

Certain plants can be grown together so that they benefit each other in some way. Such companion plants are believed to encourage beneficial insects, repel or deter pests by masking the smell of a host plant, or even sacrifice themselves by attracting pests away from a neighbouring crop.

Key companion plants
Basil has insect-repelling leaves, which are said to protect tomatoes from aphids.
Marigolds (*Tagetes*) are said to deter aphids from beans and whitefly from tomatoes.
Garlic chives have a powerful smell, which is said to protect carrots from carrot fly and can repel aphids from raspberries.
Lavender is a great draw for pollinators and its strong scent is said to confuse pests.
Nasturtium is reputed to lure aphids away from beans and brings in beneficial insects.
Coriander exudes a scent that is believed to repel aphids and carrot fly.
Borage is said to protect tomatoes from hornworm and is a great pollinator magnet.

Protecting against the elements
If plants are struggling in a heatwave, group pots together in the shade. Plants in pots are also much more susceptible to cold than those in the ground, so if hard frosts are forecast insulate plant roots by wrapping pots in bubble wrap or hessian sacking stuffed with straw. Mulching plants also helps to stop roots from freezing. Plunge small pots into the ground if you have the space. Move frost-tender plants to a sheltered spot away from frost pockets, group pots together, and wrap each plant in horticultural fleece or net-curtain material. In very wet weather move pots under cover and take away any saucers so the plants do not become waterlogged. Raising pots up onto feet or blocks of wood helps excess water drain away.

If you grow some flowering plants with and around your edible crops, they will help to bring in beneficial insects.

Stress-free watering

Watering is one of the most demanding aspects of growing plants in containers. Your crops are in only a finite amount of soil so your watering regime directly affects the quality and amount of food that you get. You need to watch your pots carefully, especially during a hot summer and at particular times, such as when plants are in fruit and require watering every day. However it is possible to make the best use of water without wasting your time or this valuable resource.

There are a number of things you can do that will help to conserve water. First, use the biggest container you can: 30–40cm (12–16in) or more in diameter and depth is ideal. Plastic pots are much better at retaining water than the more porous, terra-cotta ones, although you can use a sealant or line terra-cotta pots with plastic to improve their water-holding capabilities. Second, use loam-based potting compost for longer-term crops (e.g. fruit) and thirsty ones (e.g. tomatoes); multipurpose composts, particularly peat-based ones, drain more freely. Third, before planting you could mix in a water-retaining gel to help the compost hold on to water for longer, but don't overdo the quantities. Too much gel can push plants out of their pots and cause waterlogging. Finally, after planting, always mulch the pot. Covering the compost with a 5cm (2in) layer of stone, gravel, or organic matter significantly reduces the amount of moisture lost from the top layer of soil as well as helps to prevent the many problems exacerbated by water loss.

When deciding what to grow it's worth bearing in mind that some crops need more water than others. Leafy veg such as lettuces and fruiting crops such as tomatoes and courgettes require lots of water, while onions, garlic and shallots demand much less.

Collect and store as much rainwater as you can from your house, garage, and even shed, and help yourself and your plants by installing a drip irrigation system, especially if you have lots of pots. This delivers water exactly where the plants need it, and gradually soaks into the soil so there is no run-off or waste. Such a system will also save time because you will no longer need to carry hoses and watering cans around.

Optimum watering tips

- Check the moisture level in each pot every day during the growing season.
- Don't overwater. Keep the compost moist but not soggy and be consistent – don't flood your pots and then subject them to drought by letting them dry out. Applying a little water often is best practice.
- Group pots together to create beneficial, mutual shade.
- Always water in the evening or early in the morning so that water reaches plant roots rather than evaporating in the day. Bear in mind however that watering later in the day can attract slugs and snails to vulnerable plants such as seedlings.
- Remove any weeds in your pots at once.
- For very thirsty, deep-rooting plants, such as tomatoes, sink a pot or an upturned plastic bottle with the base cut off into the compost near the plant and water directly into it. This helps direct the water straight to where it is needed.

Drip irrigation systems are helpful if you have lots of containers or simply to save the time and worry of watering.

Always collect rainwater where you can in the garden. Having a few water butts close by will save you lugging watering cans too far between containers.

Watering with a can without a rose helps water to flow down to the roots below.

A good time of day to water is the morning, when strong sun will not cause it to evaporate; it sets plants up for the day.

Harvesting & storing crops

Harvesting is not an exact science. The length of time from sowing to cropping can depend on the variety, the weather, and where you are growing, but if you think something looks ready why not try it and see? Most crops need picking before they go past their best and to keep more produce coming. A few, such as the root vegetables carrots and parsnips and most citrus fruit, can be left in the ground or on the tree until you want them.

Nothing beats the taste of fresh, home-grown produce straight from the garden, and this is definitely the best way to enjoy your crops if you can. But if you find yourself with a glut of something there is no need to waste any of your hard-earned produce. Most fruit, vegetables, and herbs will keep in the refrigerator for a few days. Otherwise almost everything you grow can be frozen, dried, stored, or pickled, depending on the crop. Individual instructions on harvesting and storing are provided in each entry in the crop directories (see pp40–169). If you plan it right you can enjoy something delicious from your pots every month of the year.

Tomatoes will happily stay ripe on the plant until you are ready to pick them, ensuring they are always fresh.

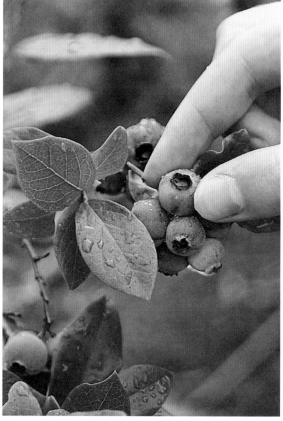

Blueberry fruit ripens at different times so keep checking plants and picking often, to ensure you don't miss any.

How to collect & save seed

Although most seed is inexpensive, the cost does add up, so to make a small financial difference to your outlay every year why not collect and save your own seed? More rewarding than any monetary gain however is the satisfaction you get in completing the circle – from crop to seed to crop again. You can also exchange seed with friends and family or get involved in some of the organized seed swaps that take place among the country's horticultural groups and allotmenteers.

Some results from home-collected seed won't be quite as predictable as they would be with shop-bought seed: for example, seed from F_1 hybrids can be tricky and it's a gamble to know what sort of crop you will get – if any at all. Seed from heritage varieties and other hybrids is much more reliable and worth collecting. Easy seeds to save include beans, peas, pumpkins and squash, tomatoes, coriander, fennel, and lettuces that have bolted.

- On a dry day collect seed – only from healthy plants.
- Remove the whole seedhead and place it in a paper bag.
- Dry it in the airing cupboard or on a windowsill before extracting the seed.
- Remove any remaining chaff from the seed, then store it somewhere cool and dry in an airtight jar. The refrigerator is better than a kitchen cupboard.
- Always label and date the seed.
- Clean seed from fleshy fruit such as tomatoes by sieving the fruit and then rinsing the pulp from the seed. Leave to dry before storing.

Right: When picking beans late in the season, leave a few on the plant to dry. Collect them for their seed before the frost.

Cut off whole seedheads of coriander. Put them in paper bags to dry, before rubbing off and storing the seeds.

Solving common problems

Growing in containers presents a unique set of challenges: you are raising plants in a limited space and have to take extra care with watering and feeding. If you get this right you will have strong, healthy, productive plants that are less vulnerable to attack and more able to stand up for themselves if attacks are made.

Always give crops the space they need; do not be tempted to overcrowd your pots in such limited growing conditions. Keep on top of the watering routine, but do not overdo it – waterlogging can cause its own troubles. Remember to feed your crops once a week during the growing season. A 5cm (2in) layer of mulch will help your plants to grow strongly and healthily.

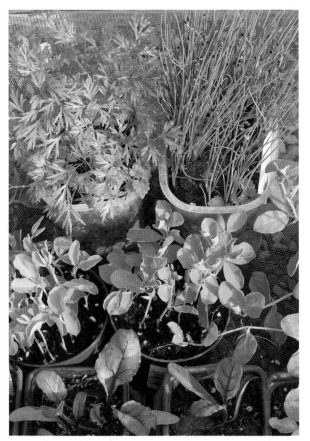

Slugs and snails can devastate seedlings and young plants so ensure the plants are adequately protected at all times.

Once you have mastered these cultural tactics, use any other precautionary measures you can to protect your plants. Barrier deterrents such as netting and fleece make an enormous difference, as does squashing or picking off insect pests such as caterpillars, aphids, slugs, and snails as soon as you spot them. Lay chicken wire or prickly-leaved plants such as holly over containers of newly sown seed or recently germinated plants to deter squirrels and mice. A few chemical treatments are available, but they can have a detrimental effect on the ecosystem of your garden, so never apply such chemicals when plants are in flower. Note the instructions for use of the pesticide, particularly on the period that must be left between treatment and harvesting.

It is impossible and therefore pointless to try to be free of all pest and disease problems in the garden; they are an inevitable and necessary part of the ecosystem. Fortunately the main culprits you will encounter are fairly predictable, so be vigilant, spot them early, and try to keep their numbers and damage to a minimum.

Slugs and snails will definitely be your most frustrating troublemakers, and the best form of defence is to try everything. Always be on the lookout for slugs and snails, and if they're getting out of hand a twilight collecting prowl can work wonders. Slug pellets, containing ferric phosphate, scattered thinly around vulnerable

Right: Covering the compost around vulnerable plants and seedlings with a thick layer of sharp grit or gravel should help in the battle against slugs and snails.

- **Copper tape** gives slugs and snails an electric shock and is ideal for wrapping around the rim of each pot. Or try smearing each rim with Vaseline.
- **Beer traps** Sink an old jam jar or yogurt pot into the compost and fill it with beer.
- **Nematodes** are natural predators that can be watered into the compost when temperatures are above 5°C (41°F).
- **Grit, gravel, crushed eggshells, or crushed seashells** Spread a thick layer of anything sharp and gritty inside the rim of the pot, between rows of seedlings, or as a mulch.
- **Citrus skins** Lay pieces of citrus-fruit rind from oranges and grapefruit face up on the surface of the compost around vulnerable plants. Simply check each morning and dispose of the slugs.

plants are an effective form of control; other pellet types are more toxic to children, pets, and wildlife. Other ideas are given in the checklist (see box above). If you use traps, dispose of your prisoners by dissolving them in salty water, by snipping them in half with secateurs, or by putting them in a bag in the rubbish bin.

Powdery mildew is the white mould that appears on both the upper and lower surfaces of leaves in dry weather. It is worse where there is poor air circulation among plants, so don't overcrowd your pots. Mulching and consistent watering will reduce stress. Look out for resistant cultivars in seed catalogues

Aphids, including blackfly and greenfly, love soft, new growth so are mainly a problem in spring, even though they are around until late summer. They will not kill your plants, but they can weaken them and also spread viruses and other diseases. Ladybirds, hoverflies, and lacewings are their natural predators, so encourage these into your garden. Aphids can also be rubbed off by hand, which is effective if there are only a few plants to treat. They can also be hosed off with insecticidal soap.

Remove snails immediately whenever you see them. This is more effective at night when they are at their most active.

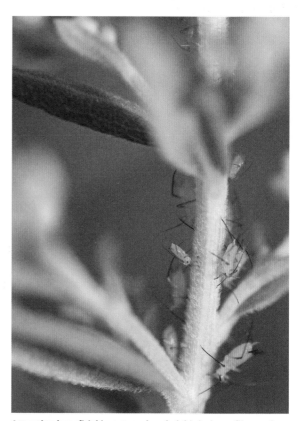

Attracting beneficial insects such as ladybirds, hoverflies, and lacewings will help to reduce aphids on your plants.

Blight is the disease most vegetable gardeners dread. This airborne fungal disease, which is common in the moist, warm conditions of late summer, affects tomatoes and potatoes and can attack the whole plant, destroying a crop very quickly. Look out for chocolate-brown blotches on the leaves and stems, which will eventually spread to the fruit or tubers and the whole plant will become slimy and black. Be vigilant and remove infected leaves immediately, although it is only a matter of time before it takes hold. Cut the stems of potatoes down to the soil surface straight away, crossing your fingers it hasn't spread to the potatoes below. Wait a couple of weeks before lifting your potatoes, to allow the skins to thicken. As soon as you spot signs of blight, pick all your tomatoes, ripe or not. When plants are infected don't compost them, but put them in bags and bin them. Resistant varieties are also available – try the 'Sarpo' range of potatoes and 'Ferline' or 'Legend' tomatoes.

Caterpillars of the cabbage white butterflies love all brassicas, such as cabbages, as well as radishes, so if you are growing these it is best to be prepared by netting the plants. Otherwise, as soon as you see the butterflies flitting round your pots, look for the eggs and squash them. Their caterpillars will be on the munch from late spring until autumn.

Beetles such as the stripy rosemary beetle love anything in the rosemary family and also eat the leaves of lavender and sage. Adults feed during late summer, and the larvae can be found on the undersides of leaves from autumn to spring. Tap them onto newspaper laid around your pots or pick them off by hand.

Flea beetles are a problem on all young brassicas, including radishes, Oriental leaves, cabbages, and rocket, peppering their leaves with holes. Damage is often worse in warm, dry weather. You may avoid attacks by growing crops in tall pots, which these flying insects cannot

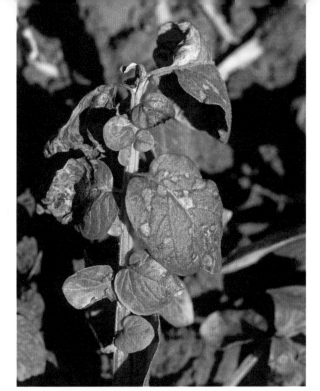

Keep an eye out for the tell-tale signs of blight from midsummer onward and particularly after rain.

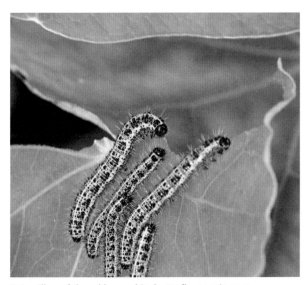

Caterpillars of the cabbage white butterfly can ruin your crop unless you cover plants with a mesh netting to stop the butterflies laying eggs on the leaves.

reach, or by covering seedlings with netting to keep the flea beetles away. If plants are attacked, paint a piece of cardboard with something sticky such as treacle or syrup. Wave it across or above the leaves, and the beetles jump off the leaves onto the cardboard, which you then discard.

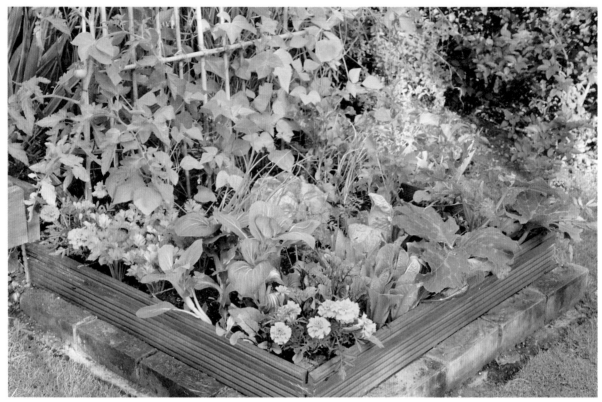

By following a few simple steps and putting some useful cultural principles into practice even seasoned vegetable growers will be surprised at how much produce they can get from such a small area.

Metre-square year-round planter

Growing your own vegetables doesn't have to be all about space. It is perfectly possible to concentrate on just a single planter 1 x 1m (3 x 3ft) and, by growing intensively and making constant use of all the space, get a fantastic yield with the minimum amount of effort.

Based on the American Square Foot gardening concept, this idea uses small areas of land for intensive vegetable growing and is ideal for large containers or square raised beds – but it doesn't even need to be a perfect square or exactly 1 x 1m (3 x 3ft). By sowing crops closer than you normally would and immediately replacing each crop with a different one as soon as it's harvested, you can enjoy maximum yield in the minimum time and space. Such concentrated growing

means there are fewer gaps for weeds to colonize and the intensive plant coverage acts as a living mulch, helping to retain water and prevent weeds. Thus maintenance tasks are quicker and easier than with a large site.

You can grow absolutely anything, but why not try a simple selection of catch crops of leaves (for example, pak choi, lettuces, spinach), beetroot, carrots, spring onions, and radishes with courgettes, a row of beans, and a tomato plant inside a raised bed of 1 x 1m (3 x 3ft).

You do need a patch of ground for this project, as well as sufficient room around it to reach across the bed to sow, weed, water, and harvest, so you can avoid walking on the soil.

The raised bed should be in a sunny spot so that it gets maximum light. Fill it with the best soil you can get, mixing in plenty of garden compost or well-rotted organic matter. It's a good idea to add slow-release fertilizer too, to give your crops the best possible start. After this initial preparation the plot is not dug again, thus helping to preserve the soil structure and also entailing less work.

Spacing and sowing crops

Seed is station sown where possible, which means that you sow at the correct final spacings and don't spend time thinning out later. You also plant in squares, not rows, giving equal space between individual plants; thus they can be grown closer than normal. When using miniature or compact varieties you can plant even closer and get a greater yield, even if the crops are sometimes of a smaller size. The number of plants grown in each square depends on the crop, and some crops may occupy more than one square. In one square for example you can grow: 16 beetroots or carrots; or six spinach plants; or two beans; but only a single courgette. Some larger plants, such as courgettes, will eventually take up more than one square, but in the meantime use the surrounding squares for faster-growing crops such as radishes or salad leaves.

Start sowing in spring with early, fast-growing crops in each square. These can be harvested in time for a second sowing, by which time it's safe to sow more tender plants such as courgettes. Make the best use of space by growing plants that climb up supports: beans, peas, tomatoes, squash, pumpkins, cucumbers, even some types of courgette can all be grown vertically. Just

make sure you plant them at the northern end of your bed so that shade is cast away from the rest of the crops. If there is space add in some companion plants (see p27).

Optimal use

Once a crop is harvested, clear it away and sprinkle in slow-release fertilizer at the same time as digging fresh garden compost or manure into its square. Then sow a new crop. This makes optimum use of each space by never leaving any patches of bare soil idle. It also means you are constantly improving the soil in the raised bed.

METRE-SQUARE CHECKLIST

- This technique is suitable for practically all crops. Just bear in mind that some of them, such as onions, are in the ground for a long time, while others, such as brassicas, occupy a lot of space.

- Plant bushy crops such as peppers, chillies, and some types of courgette at the bed corners so they do not take over the plot.

- Although the raised bed requires regular attention, maintenance is minimal. When tackled a square at a time, the tending of such small spaces takes minutes rather than hours, and the intensive culture creates a microclimate that conserves moisture and keeps weeds down, meaning even less work.

- Add garden compost and slow-release fertilizer at every harvest so you are improving the soil throughout the season.

- Extending the season is simple. Either warm the whole bed with black plastic sheeting in early spring before sowing or concentrate on individual squares by placing bell cloches just where they are needed. Fleece can be laid over late crops to protect them against cold weather.

Planting your metre-square year-round planter

What you need
- raised bed, 1 x 1m (3 x 3ft);
- garden soil or loam-based potting compost; ■ garden compost; ■ measuring tape;
- hammer, nails; ■ garden twine; ■ variety of vegetable seed (see p36); ■ bamboo canes; ■ cordon tomato plant

1 Fill the raised bed with two parts garden soil and one part garden compost mixed together. Then using the measuring tape divide the raised bed into a grid of evenly sized squares; this bed has 16 squares of 25 x 25cm (10 x 10in). Tap in nails at each point.

2 Run the garden twine between the marker nails across the bed and knot each end tightly once it is taut. Then water the bed using a hose or watering can with a rose so it is ready for sowing.

6 Harvest your crops when they are ready. As each square empties, fork a trowelful of fresh garden compost and some slow-release fertilizer into it and re-sow. These radishes were in and out before the courgette required more room to grow.

7 Once all frosts have passed other more tender crops can be sown. Allocate four squares in a corner for a single courgette, sowing it in the corner square to give the plant maximum space to spread out. This is a patio variety, which worked particularly well here.

8 Make a framework of bamboo canes for your beans and sow a row along the three squares at the back of the raised bed, saving the fourth square for the cordon tomato.

3 Before sowing your first crops work out the appropriate number of seeds for each crop in its allocated square – one, four, six, nine, or 16 seeds may fit in the square, depending on the crop. Then make sure that each seed is evenly spaced within the square.

4 Water in the seed well. A watering can with a rose is perfect for this because you can concentrate on each square one at a time as necessary.

5 If slugs and snails are a problem (see p32) try to deter them for example by sticking a strip of copper tape around the rim of the raised bed. Both slugs and snails hate the feel of it and should leave your precious plants alone. Feed and water the plants regularly.

9 Plant a cordon tomato in its allocated square and tie it to its own cane for support. Continue tying in and pinching out sideshoots on the tomato throughout the summer.

10 You can add some companion plants at the corners and around the tomato. This may help to bring in pollinating insects for your flowering crops and encourage ladybirds, which feed on pests such as aphids that can damage crops.

11 Keep harvesting your crops as soon as they are ready. Depending on the crops you can keep refreshing the compost and re-sowing well into summer, and you should then still be harvesting right up until the first frosts.

Fruit

Apples

Thanks to dwarf rootstocks apple trees fare very happily in containers – you do not need an orchard to harvest your own sweet, crisp apples. There are hundreds of different varieties so the first thing you need to decide is whether you want to eat the apples or cook with them. If you have the space why not try both, but make sure your chosen varieties flower at the same time so they can pollinate each other. If you want to grow only one tree, select a variety that is self-fertile or try a family tree – one that has two or more varieties grafted onto the trunk, giving you a different apple on each main branch.

Basic needs

Use a pot 45–50cm (18–20in) in diameter with loam-based potting compost mixed with grit. Half-barrels are good.

Growing techniques

1 Look for a named cultivar that has been specially grown for a container and has been grafted onto 'M26' or 'M9' rootstock (see p44).

2 Plant bare-root trees in the dormant season between autumn and late winter; container-grown plants can be planted at any time. Water well and place in a warm, sheltered site.

3 Work rootgrow or general-purpose fertilizer

such as blood, fish, and bone into the planting hole. Stake the tree (see p44–45). Then mulch.

4 Keep an eye on watering, particularly in dry spells and when the fruit starts to swell.

If growing apples in a frost-prone area choose later flowering varieties to prevent frost damage.

An apple tree can be grown as a single-stem cordon where space is limited.

5 From spring onward feed every two weeks with a balanced liquid feed.

6 Topdress in winter with manure.

Problem solving

Apples are susceptible to damage from codling moths. They also suffer from fungal diseases such as apple scab, where damage is generally only skin deep and can be peeled away. Some varieties offer resistance to apple scab. Wet summers cause brown rot: discard infected fruit when you see it. Erratic watering can cause sunken holes in fruit, known as bitter pit; fortunately affected fruit can still be eaten.

Harvesting and storage

Windfalls on the ground or in the container are a good sign fruit is ripe. Pick by cupping an apple and twisting it on its stem – there should be no need to pull. Different varieties are ready at different times, and if you choose your trees carefully you can harvest over a long period. Early varieties are ready from midsummer and must be eaten fairly quickly as they do not store well. Others are harvested in mid-autumn, and these can be stored in a cool garage or shed. When storing apples do not let them touch, and check regularly for spoiling and rotting. Apples can also be puréed and frozen, or slow dried in the oven before storing.

VARIETIES cooking: 'Arthur Turner', 'Emneth Early'; eating: 'Discovery', 'Pixie', 'Sunset'

Expert tips

- Plant a pot-grown tree at the same depth as previously. If a bare-root tree, look for the soil mark on the stem (see p45).

- Pot on every other year in autumn, cutting off any thick roots. Once in its final pot, refresh potting compost every year, giving the tree a root prune every alternate year.

- Unless you choose a self-fertile variety or family tree, you need to grow more than one tree. Trees are grouped according to pollination so grow trees in the same or adjoining group. Seek advice from a specialist nursery when buying.

- Pruning depends on the way your tree has been trained and where it fruits – either on branch spurs or tips. Minarettes (single, vertical-stemmed cordons) are ideal for containers, taking up little room and needing minimal pruning. It is simplest to buy a tree already trained to shape; the main leader can be reduced in spring, if necessary, and new side branches pruned back to three leaves in summer. Thin the stems while the tree is dormant in winter to maintain the formative shape and to keep an open branch structure.

Early apples can be eaten straight from the tree, while later cropping varieties will benefit from storage first.

Apple harvest

Apples are the most popular fruit tree grown and on the right rootstock will thrive in a pot. A simple, single-stemmed cordon looks stunning laden with sweet, refreshing fruit and takes up very little space, so is perfect for a small yard or garden. There are hundreds of varieties to choose from, but go for one that is not readily available in the shops or, even better, buy one that has some sort of historical connection to your area.

When selecting any fruit tree it is important that you consider its rootstock, but when growing in containers the rootstock choice is absolutely vital. You need an 'M26' or 'M9' rootstock. Do not go for the very dwarfing rootstocks; although they are small, growing them in a container puts them under even more stress. Having settled on your choice of rootstock you then need to decide which apple variety you want to grow (see p43). This can be a little tricky if you want only one tree, as it must be self-fertile (see p42).

Bare-root and container-grown plants can be planted at different times of year (see p42). Give trees a sunny, sheltered spot so that fruit has the maximum chance of growing and ripening.

Staking will help to anchor the roots and stop windrock. Use a stake that is only one third the height of the tree so that the stem can still sway in the wind and gradually thicken. Insert the stake on the side of the prevailing wind so the tree is blown away from the stake. Make sure the stake is firmly in the potting compost or else it will not anchor the tree. Check the tree tie regularly to make sure that it is not too tight and loosen it as the tree trunk expands.

Keep your tree well watered in dry weather and when the fruit begins to swell. A good mulch will help it to retain moisture as will topdressing the tree with garden compost or well-rotted farmyard manure every spring. Water plants regularly with a balanced liquid fertilizer.

An apple tree is an investment for the future, and although it may take a little while for your tree to reach full productivity it will be well worth the wait.

Planting your apple tree

What you need

- bare-root apple tree;
- terra-cotta pot at least 40cm (16in) wide and deep;
- horticultural grit;
- loam-based potting compost;
- fertilizer (see p15);
- stake and tree tie.

1 Unpack your apple tree as soon as it arrives. Place it in a bucket of water so the roots do not dry out. At potting time take a good look at your tree to establish exactly where the graft union is – it is the swollen part where the variety has been joined to the rootstock. This must be well above the surface of the compost after planting.

2 Put a layer of drainage material in the bottom of the pot and then half fill it with potting compost. Mix in some fertilizer and place the tree on top. Insert the stake carefully in-between the roots before filling in with compost. Keep adding compost, firming it down as you go until the tree is stable and the graft union is still above the soil level.

3 Secure the stake to the tree with the tree tie, placing a spacer between the tree stem and the stake to stop them rubbing against each other.

4 Water the tree in well and then mulch with well-rotted manure or garden compost. Top up the mulch if the level drops after watering. Feed and water regularly.

5 Warm weather will encourage your tree to blossom. If hard frosts are forecast, protect the flowers and very young fruit to ensure you still get a good crop.

Pears

Although pears are a little tricky to grow, the taste of home-grown fruit is a world away from what we have become accustomed to from the supermarket. If you are short on space, try a family pear tree, which has two or more varieties grafted onto the trunk, or choose one of the self-fertile varieties, although these do even better when grown with a compatible partner. Always go for the dwarf container rootstock 'Quince C' when growing in pots.

Basic needs

Use a pot 45–50cm (18–20in) in diameter with loam-based potting compost mixed with grit.

Growing techniques

1 In autumn plant at the same level that the tree was in the previous pot or in the ground.

2 Water well, then place the pot in a sunny, sheltered site, well away from any frost pockets.

3 Refresh the top layer of potting compost in spring, sprinkling in slow-release fertilizer and mulching with well-rotted manure. Keep the mulch away from the trunk.

4 Feed once a week in the growing season with a balanced liquid fertilizer.

5 Water well in dry weather and as fruit swells.

6 Prune every year in winter and summer.

Expert tips

- For an early crop buy a three-year-old tree.
- Almost all pears are spur fruiting and can be grown as standards or trained as cordons or espaliers. Prune single cordons by reducing the main leader in spring, then prune side branches to three leaves in midsummer, and thin fruiting stems to 10cm (4in) apart in winter.

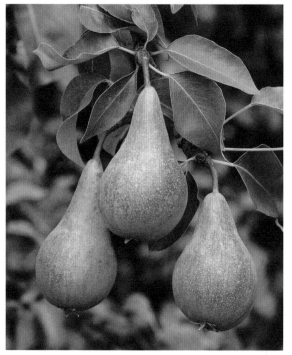

For the best-sized fruits thin pears in summer back to two or three fruit per cluster.

Problem solving

Disease resistance in individual cultivars may differ, but always look out for brown rot, particularly in wet summers. Prune out any infected fruit to prevent it spreading. The common pear leaf blister mite causes black blisters on leaves but is mainly cosmetic.

Harvesting and storage

Pears are ready for harvesting when they are firm but have changed colour slightly; they should come off the tree with a gentle lift and twist. If gathered too early they will not ripen; if too late they can rot or taste gritty. After picking store pears in a cool, dark place until ripe. Early cultivars take a week to ripen; later ones a few months.

VARIETIES 'Beth', 'Beurré Hardy', 'Catillac', 'Concorde', 'Conference', 'Doyenne du Comice'

Figs

Figs are possibly the perfect crop for growing in pots, because they love having their growth kept in check. Beautifully architectural, with stunning foliage, they make lovely features on a terrace or deck. In cool-temperate areas just make sure you choose one of the hardier cultivars to ensure you get a good crop.

Basic needs
Use a pot 35–40cm (14–16in) in diameter filled with nutrient-rich, loam-based potting compost mixed with grit so it drains freely.

This large fig may ripen during summer; the small figs won't, nor will they survive winter. The figs that do overwinter are tiny, and even they may not develop if it is very cold.

Growing techniques
1 Position figs against the warmest, sunniest wall you have to maximize the available heat and light.

2 Keep well watered so the soil never dries out.

Expert tips
- Open, goblet-shaped bushes are the easiest shape for pot-grown figs.
- Before growth starts in spring, cut out any dead and weak branches. Summer prune by nipping out the shoot tips at the ends of all new growth, leaving five leaves per branch. Always wear gloves when pruning to protect your hands against the irritating, milky sap from fig stems.
- Water regularly, particularly in summer.
- In spring replace the top few centimetres of potting compost.
- By the end of the summer you may have a few different-sized fruit on your plant. The largest should soon be ready to pick and the very smallest will develop into next year's harvest. Take off those in-between.

3 Mulch in spring with well-rotted organic matter. In summer apply liquid fertilizer every week.

4 In cool-temperate climates move the fig to a frost-free place for the winter. Otherwise insulate the pot with bubble wrap or horticultural fleece.

5 Pot on every couple of years in spring.

Problem solving
Net plants against birds.

Harvesting and storage
You can smell when figs are ready. They are fragrant and soft to handle, but the longer you wait the sweeter your figs will be. Hold the fruit by the stalk and pull it gently away from the stem. Eat fresh or slowly dry them in the oven.

VARIETIES 'Brown Turkey', 'Brunswick', 'Petite Nigra', 'White Ischia', 'White Marseilles'

Citrus

All members of the citrus family – lemons, limes, grapefruits, kumquats, oranges, and calamondins – are frost tender and need consistently warm temperatures. In cool-temperate regions, grow citrus in a conservatory. Choose light, plastic rather than heavier, clay pots to make this annual task easier. Getting growing conditions right is vital, but other than this citrus plants are really not difficult fruit to grow. They are beautiful, small trees with fragrant flowers blossoming throughout the year, and there is something special about picking your own lemons or oranges that makes any extra effort entirely worthwhile.

Basic needs

Pick a pot 50cm (20in) or more in diameter for a two- to three-year-old plant. Mix 20 percent grit or sharp sand into loam-based potting compost or use a specialist citrus potting compost. Use ericaceous potting compost if you live in a hard-water area and cannot water with rainwater.

Growing techniques

1 For plants to fruit well, the right conditions are key. Citrus needs a long, hot, humid growing season, with at least six months at 14°C (57°F) for fruit to ripen, and a frost-free winter with minimum temperatures of 15°C (59°F). Plants become dormant in temperatures lower than this; and if below 7°C (45°F) they may die.

2 To increase the chances of fruiting, purchase mature plants, because citrus is extremely slow to grow from cuttings or seed.

3 Plant citrus trees in spring.

4 Water well, keeping the compost moist, because a lack of water can cause fruit to drop. Rainwater is best if you can collect it. Keep plants

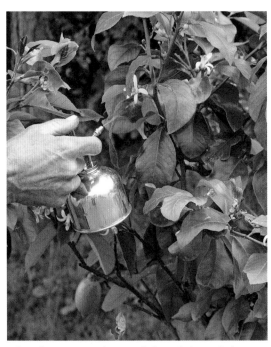

In hot, dry summers mist around plants during and after flowering to help increase humidity.

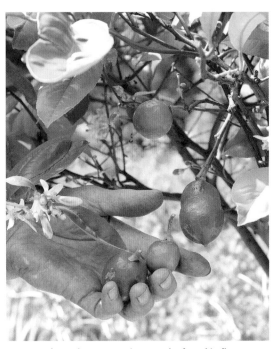

Between the various types, citrus can be found in flower almost year-round. It takes up to a year for fruit to ripen.

Expert tips

- Citrus needs minimal pruning, especially if you are growing dwarf, container varieties. Remove shoots below the graft union on the main stem and pinch out the tips of vigorous growth in summer. In late winter reshape plants by thinning out any overcrowded branches and cutting back leggy branches by two thirds. Beware savage thorns.

- Stand pots on saucers of wet gravel to raise humidity levels. Misting leaves in summer also helps.

- The warmer the temperature the better the fruit tastes.

Citrus grown in pots should be placed in a warm, sunny spot in summer and then, in cool-temperate areas, moved into a frost-free environment to overwinter.

almost dry in winter and then as temperatures begin to warm up start watering with tepid water to encourage flowering. Allow excess water to drain away so the plant does not sit in it.

5 Refresh the top 5cm (2in) of potting compost in spring. Every three or four years repot in spring when the roots become congested.

6 Citrus are hungry plants, so feed them throughout the year. From early spring to mid-autumn give plants high-nitrogen fertilizer followed by a balanced winter feed. Specialist citrus feeds are also available.

Problem solving

Most problems such as failing to flower, losing flowers early, yellow leaves, or leaf drop are caused by giving plants the wrong conditions. Insufficient light, food, water, or humidity and too low temperatures can all cause problems, so take care not to overwater in winter, avoid fluctuating temperatures, and keep humidity levels high.

Harvesting and storage

Fruit can be picked when ripe or left on the tree. Cut off with secateurs leaving a short stalk. Undamaged fruit can be stored somewhere cool and dry for several weeks, made into preserves, or can be bottled.

VARIETIES clementine: *C. reticulata* Mandarin Group 'Nules'; grapefruit: *C.* x *paradisi* 'Marsh'; lemon: *C.* x *meyeri* 'Meyer', *C. limon* 'Garey's Eureka'; orange: *C. sinensis* 'Washington'; Persian lime: *C. aurantiifolia* 'Tahiti'; satsuma: *C. unshiu* 'Owari'

Cherries

Cherries are stunning fruit trees. Dripping blossom in spring then dangling fruit in summer they often end the season with vibrant autumn colour. There are two types of cherry – sweet or sour. Sweet cherries are best eaten fresh, while sour cherries need cooking before they become delicious enough to eat. All sour cherries are self-fertile, but some sweet cherries are not; in these cases seek advice from a specialist nursery to ensure you buy varieties that can pollinate each other. Select dwarfing rootstocks to keep trees at a manageable height of 2–3m (6¹/₂–10ft). 'Table' is a perfect rootstock for sweet cherries in pots, 'Colt' for the less vigorous sour. Grow as bushes or fan train.

If you need to protect cherry blossom against frost with fleece be sure to remove it in the day for foraging bees.

Basic needs
Give trees a large pot, 60cm (2ft) or more wide, filled with loam-based potting compost.

Growing techniques
1 Plant as bare-root or container plants between late autumn and early spring. Sweet cherries need full sun; sour cherries tolerate more shade.

2 Cherries are shallow-rooting and will dry out quickly in pots so water trees well after planting. Watering is also especially important while fruit is first growing and during dry periods.

3 Refresh the top layer of potting compost every spring, sprinkling in a balanced, slow-release fertilizer. Give a balanced liquid feed in summer.

4 Blossom comes early in the season so place the pot in a sheltered site. Protect flowers and fruit from frost with fleece; remove the cover as soon as possible to allow access to pollinating insects.

Problem solving
Bacterial canker, seen as brown spots on leaves and the eventual die-back of branches, can kill, so cut out any affected branches and use a copper-based fungicide in late summer. Reduce the chances of silver leaf by pruning in summer. Protect the ripe fruit from birds with netting.

Harvesting and storage
From midsummer onwards, pick cherries by their stalks. Sweet cherries are best eaten when fresh but will keep in the refrigerator for a week. Sour cherries need cooking. Cherries can also be frozen whole (removing stones first) or puréed.

VARIETIES sour: 'Meteor', 'Morello', 'Nabella'; sweet: 'Merchant', 'Stella', 'Summer Sun'

Expert tips

- Sweet cherries fruit on one- and two-year-old stems. Shorten new shoots in summer to encourage the fruiting spurs.

- Sour cherries fruit on wood formed the previous year. Prune out whole shoots in summer to reduce overcrowding and stimulate new growth.

Peaches

A home-grown peach picked fresh from the tree has a taste delectably different from any others you will have tasted. Unfortunately all that taste and evocative aroma need a bit of effort, especially in cool-temperate climates. Peach trees are hardy, but their flowers are not. Go for genetically dwarf, compact types, known as patio peaches, or any conventional type grown on a container rootstock such as 'Pixy' or 'St Julien A'. These are easier to tend.

Basic needs
Start young trees in a 20cm (8in) pot filled with loam-based potting compost mixed with grit.

Growing techniques
1 Plant either bare-root or container-grown plants in autumn, placing them against a warm, sunny, sheltered wall. Water them very well.

2 As blossom appears feed with a balanced liquid fertilizer every couple of weeks. Water regularly.

3 Give the developing fruit room to grow by gradually thinning them out to 5cm (2in) apart.

4 In spring refresh the compost and mulch.

5 Repot every other year into a larger pot. A final pot of 40cm (16in) diameter should be sufficient.

Problem solving
Peach leaf curl is a common fungal disease that distorts leaves with vivid, pink blisters. It is spread by rain splash, so cover containers between mid-winter and late spring. 'Avalon Pride' is reputed to be resistant to this disease.

In cool-temperate areas cover peach blossom with fleece to protect it against frost.

Peaches don't all ripen at once, so keep checking the tree for ripened fruit to pick.

Harvesting and storage
Fruit is ripe when perfumed and soft; pick it regularly. Eat fresh or make into jam or chutney.

VARIETIES 'Avalon Pride', 'Bonanza', 'Duke of York', 'Garden Annie', 'Garden Lady', 'Peregrine', 'Red Haven', 'Rochester'

Expert tips

- If growing in a cool-temperate climate choose cultivars that flower late.

- Otherwise use fleece to protect flowers from frost by night; remove the covering by day to allow access to pollinators.

- Increase fruiting potential by pollinating plants yourself with a soft brush.

- Peaches flower on the previous year's growth so need replacement pruning to produce new wood every year. Prune out old shoots to a narrow growth bud. Compact types need little pruning – just cut out dead, diseased, or damaged wood.

- To prevent silver leaf and canker prune only on a dry, sunny day in spring or summer.

Plums

Grow your own and you get to choose between plums, damsons, gages, or bullaces, or plant one of each. They are close relatives, although damsons and bullaces have smaller, tarter fruit that tastes better cooked. There are many self-fertile varieties, but you will have a better crop if you grow two trees from the same or adjacent pollination groups. Go for plants grafted onto the semi-dwarfing 'Pixy' rootstock and train them as open bushes, pyramids, or fans if they have not already been grown in that shape.

Basic needs
Use a 60cm (24in) pot with plenty of drainage holes – plums hate sitting in wet soil. Fill it with loam-based potting compost mixed with grit.

Growing techniques
1 Plant as bare-root or pot-grown plants in mid-autumn, ensuring trees are inserted at same level as in the previous pot or ground. Water well.

2 Position the pot in a warm, sunny spot.

3 Plums are thirsty trees, so water well in the first year while they establish; also water in dry spells.

4 Give pots a mulch with well-rotted manure every spring to retain moisture. Feed regularly.

5 Plums are early flowering and although the trees are hardy the flowers are not. Be ready to protect flowers and fruit with fleece on frosty nights, removing it for pollinators the next day.

6 Improve yields by thinning plums to 7.5cm (3in) apart when they are small.

Problem solving
Keep pruning to a minimum to avoid silver leaf and bacterial canker; when necessary prune in spring or midsummer. Wasps and birds can be a nuisance so net trees and hang wasp traps. Fruit can also be attacked by maggots of the plum

Expert tips

- Initially prune to produce a framework of strong, open branches. After this prune only to remove dead or damaged wood and take out suckers.
- If you have room for only one tree, assist in its pollination by rubbing the flowers with a small brush.

moth or sawfly moth. Erect pheromone traps or spray with a pesticide containing deltamethrin or lambda-cyhalothrin.

Harvesting and storage
All taste best if left to ripen on the tree. Fruit is ready when coloured and emitting a sweet, heavy scent. Windfalls are also a good clue. Eat fresh or de-stone and freeze whole or puréed, or make into jam, chutney, or wine.

VARIETIES bullace: 'Shepherd's Bullace'; damson: 'Farleigh Damson'; gage: 'Cambridge Gage'; plum: 'Blue Tit', 'Opal', 'Victoria'

Mature plum fruit have a distinctive dusty coating, or bloom, that can be rubbed off easily with your fingers.

Olives

As olive trees are evocative for some people of summer holidays and lazy days, having your own tree can be immensely satisfying, particularly if it produces fruit. These slow-growing trees have excellent ornamental properties and in a warm, sheltered position, or in a warm-temperate climate, established trees may produce a crop of olives.

Basic needs
Good drainage is vital so mix grit with loam-based potting compost. Start off young olive trees in a 30–35cm (12–14in) pot.

Growing techniques
1 Grow from young plants, planted in autumn in a sheltered, sunny spot – against a warm house wall is ideal. Stake each tree firmly and water well.

2 Although olives are drought tolerant, you must still water regularly, ensuring the potting compost

By growing more than one cultivar of olive you can greatly improve the yield.

is moist in dry spells. Reduce watering during winter, but do not allow the potting compost to dry out because it will inhibit flowering later on.

3 Apply a balanced liquid feed monthly during the growing season.

Expert tips

- Olives require little pruning; just thin out branches in spring to keep an open centre and prune the tips of the main branches every year after flowering to strong replacement shoots.

- Although most olive trees are self-fertile growing more than one cultivar will help pollination and give a more reliable yield.

- Thin out crops to three or four fruit every 30cm (12in) to help them ripen well and avoid early fruit drop.

- Protect plant roots from frosts in cold areas by insulating pots with fleece or bubble wrap and straw. Trees will be damaged by temperatures that drop below -10°C (14°F).

Problem solving
Prolonged exposure to the cold can cause splitting bark, die-back, and leaf drop. Plants should regrow, but crops and growth will be affected that season. Scale insects can sometimes be a problem, but this is mainly a cosmetic one. Wipe them off as soon as they are discovered.

Harvesting and storage
Olives can be picked when firm and black and eaten raw, although they won't taste like the shop-bought ones you are used to (these are dehydrated in salt and stored in olive oil or brine).

VARIETIES 'Africana', 'Aglandau', 'Cailletier', 'El Greco', 'Frantoio', 'Mission', 'Sativa'

Gooseberries

Now undergoing something of resurgence in popularity, gooseberries are old-fashioned fruit with a sweet, sharp punch. They are hardy, easy, and self-fertile so you need grow only one plant if space is limited. Gooseberries are available as bushes or trained as cordons or standards, which are perfect for containers because they are very productive but take up little space.

Basic needs

Loam-based potting compost provides stability and water retention. Mix with grit, for good drainage, in a pot 30cm (12in) or more deep.

Growing techniques

1 Plant as bare-root or container-grown plants between late autumn and early spring, in a sheltered, sunny spot, although plants still fruit – just less – in shade. Water well, then mulch the roots to conserve the water.

2 Water well as fruit starts to swell and during very dry spells of weather.

3 Feed every couple of weeks from spring onward, with a balanced liquid fertilizer.

4 Protect flowering plants with fleece against frost.

Problem solving

Poor air circulation causes powdery mildew (see p34), although resistant varieties such as 'Invicta' are available. Sawfly caterpillars can defoliate plants in no time so be vigilant from spring onward; remove any you see at once.

Birds love gooseberries so cover plants tautly with netting.

Pick the first gooseberries when they are not fully ripe in late spring, leaving the rest to ripen fully for picking later on.

Bullfinches love the buds and blackbirds the sweet berries; net plants if birds are a nuisance.

Harvesting and storage

Gooseberries are best thinned in late spring when they are not quite ripe; harvest every other fruit and use them for jam making. Pick the rest in summer. Wear gloves – the thorns are savage.

VARIETIES 'Greenfinch', 'Invicta', 'Leveller'

Expert tip

- To grow a cordon choose a strong branch to be the leader and clean off any shoots on its bottom 15cm (6in). Then tie it to a cane. Cut back all other shoots to two buds. The following summer re-tie the leader and prune new growth to five leaves. That winter reduce the leader by one third and shorten all other shoots back to two buds. Do this every year.

Raspberries

Raspberries are delightfully easy and so low maintenance they can almost be ignored once planted. There are both summer- and autumn-fruiting types. If you have room grow a pot of each for a long, delicious season.

Basic needs
Three plants should grow happily in a 30cm (12in) pot. Mix grit with rich, loam-based potting compost for good drainage.

Growing techniques
1 Plant as bare-root or pot-grown plants, in mid-autumn (see p59). Insert the plant so the soil mark on its canes is at ground level. This will encourage the production of lots of new canes.

2 Water, then place in a sunny, sheltered spot.

3 Mulch plants to conserve moisture.

4 Train canes up bamboo poles (see p59) or tie twine around them to stop them flopping.

5 Keep plants well fed and watered in summer.

Problem solving
Raspberries are affected by viruses and fungal diseases, which weaken plants and affect yields. Grow certified virus-free plants, keep on top of watering and feeding, and do not crowd plants. Good air circulation is vital. Dry patches on fruit with maggots inside are evidence of raspberry beetle. There is no cure; autumn varieties are less susceptible. Birds can also be a

Autumn-fruiting raspberry stems are cut down in late winter and reshoot in spring.

If raspberries are ripe they should separate cleanly from the plant. Pick when the weather is dry.

Expert tips

- Summer raspberries fruit on growth from the year before, so cut back old canes after harvesting (see p59).

- Autumn varieties fruit on growth made in the current year. Wait until late winter to cut all the canes down. Thin out new canes in summer to stop overcrowding.

- Plants last about 10 years before becoming tired; then replace with new canes or root suckers of your own plants.

nuisance, although they do seem to find yellow-fruited varieties less palatable. Net the crops.

Harvesting and storage
Fruit should pull off the plant easily. Pick often to encourage further fruiting and prevent any missed fruit rotting and causing disease. Eat fresh or freeze, make into jams, or bottle.

VARIETIES autumn-fruiting: 'All Gold', 'Autumn Bliss'; summer-fruiting: 'Glen Ample', 'Glen Moy', 'Malling Jewel'

Raspberry perfection

Raspberries are a popular, home-grown crop and for very good reason – they are simple to grow, rewarding, and absolutely delicious. They grow well in pots and make handsome plants dripping with fruit.

When choosing your raspberry plants remember there are two types – summer and autumn fruiting.

Only autumn fruiters will give you a crop in their first year, since they fruit on the current year's growth. Their stems are all cut down in the winter after they have finished fruiting, and new ones will sprout in spring to fruit again that autumn. Summer-fruiting raspberries develop fruit on stems that grew the year before and so will not fruit until about 18 months after planting.

Plant bare-root raspberries in the dormant season and immediately cut summer-fruiting varieties down to 20cm (8in) above the surface of the potting compost. When the new growth appears in spring tie it into supports. Canes fruit only once so cut them down after harvesting to make room for the new growth.

Once you have sussed this pruning routine, raspberries are fantastically easy to grow provided that you give them a sunny, sheltered spot and regular food, and mulch them to help the potting compost retain water.

In a pot either construct a framework of bamboo canes to support your raspberries or train plants against a wall.

Planting your raspberries

What you need

- 3 or 4 x raspberry canes, preferably bare-root;
- bucket of water;
- large pot, 30cm (12in) or 40cm (16in) in diameter;
- multipurpose potting compost;
- drainage material (see p15);
- secateurs;
- bamboo canes and twine.

1 Unpack your bare-root canes as soon as they arrive and remove all their tags and packaging. Soak them in water for a couple of hours to rehydrate them and to reduce any further shock at planting. Fill the pot three quarters full of potting compost over some crocks for drainage.

2 Plant quite shallowly, covering the roots with just 8cm (3½in) of compost. Set three canes in a 30cm (12in) pot, four in a 40cm (16in) one. Water well and mulch. After planting summer-fruiting raspberries, shorten the canes back to 20cm (8in) above the soil level. Water regularly during the growing season.

3 When the new shoots on summer raspberries appear in spring remove the old canes. Add a bamboo frame to the pot for support and tie in the young raspberry canes for cropping the following year.

4 Raspberry flowers are self-fertile and will be visited by bees and other pollinating insects in spring, enabling plants to set fruit. Encourage healthy growth by feeding plants each year in spring.

5 Fruit is ripe when it separates from the plant leaving behind a clean plug. Keep picking to stimulate the development of more new fruit. When fruiting is over, cut down all these old fruiting canes.

Blueberries

Blueberries are deliciously sweet with a slight tang and so nutritious that they are celebrated as a 'superfood'. They are also attractive plants with vivid autumn colour and pretty bell flowers. Blueberries are perfect candidates for growing in containers, where you have total control over their conditions, because they are fussy, needing sun, and acid, moist, well-drained soil. Give blueberries the right conditions and your plants will thrive.

Basic needs

Use ericaceous potting compost, which is acidic, mixed with grit to help drainage (see p63). Start young plants in pots 30cm (12in) in diameter.

Growing techniques

1 Plant as bare-root or container plants in autumn or early spring. Then water each plant thoroughly.

2 Position the pot in a sheltered site where there is plenty of sun.

3 Keep the potting compost moist, but not waterlogged; nor should you let it dry out. If you can, water with rainwater rather than alkaline tap water, which will gradually neutralize the potting compost and reduce your crop. If you have to use tap water, topdress your pot with sulphur to maintain the acidic conditions.

4 Mulch plants with ericaceous materials such as bark, leafmould, or pine needles to lock in moisture around the roots.

5 Feed blueberry plants every month during the growing season with lime-free liquid fertilizer.

6 Blueberries are not totally hardy, hating the combination of cold and wet. In winter wrap pots with hessian or straw to protect plant roots against frost. In spring insulate flowers against late frosts by covering them with fleece.

7 Pot on every other year until you reach a final pot size of 40–50cm (16–20in) or more wide. After that, repot in fresh potting compost every 2–3 years.

Problem solving

Blueberries are comparatively trouble-free to grow, although birds are their biggest problem. Net plants if the birds get too greedy (see p63). Container plants are susceptible to powdery

Blueberries are such attractive plants they can hold their own beautifully with ornamental species such as this feather grass (*Stipa tenuissima*).

Blueberries are ripe when they are an even blue with a distinctive, white bloom.

mildew (see p34), which is a common problem when plants are too dry. Nip out any infected growth when you see it so it does not spread. You also need to improve your watering regime to prevent it from happening in the first place. Do this by mulching the plant and watering more regularly so the compost is always moist.

Harvesting and storage

Fruit is ready to pick when it is a deep, dark blue, from midsummer onwards. Pick over the plant several times as the fruit ripens gradually rather than all at the same time. Eat it fresh. You freeze or make blueberries into jams or preserves.

VARIETIES early: 'Spartan'; midseason: 'Bluecrop' (self-fertile), 'Chippewa' (self-fertile), 'Northcountry' (self-fertile), 'Northsky' (self-fertile), 'Sunshine Blue' (self-fertile); late: 'Chandler' (self-fertile), 'Duke'

Expert tips

- A few blueberry cultivars are self-pollinating, but they are generally more productive when grown alongside two cross-pollinating partners. Three bushes should give you an ample crop.

- Do not worry about pruning in the first two years; just keep the plants open, and cut out dead, damaged, or diseased branches. After this prune in winter when plants are dormant. Remove a quarter of the dominant shoots and about half the weaker shoots to promote stronger growth.

- Place a saucer under each pot during the growing season to stop the potting compost drying out and losing nutrients. Remove it in winter so the plant does not become waterlogged.

Irresistible blueberries

Blueberries are picky plants demanding moist, light, acid soil to thrive. They are therefore the perfect crop for a pot, where you can give them exactly what they need. They are also fine-looking plants with attractive flowers, autumn leaf colours, and mouth watering fruit, and they provide a great display in even the simplest terra-cotta pot.

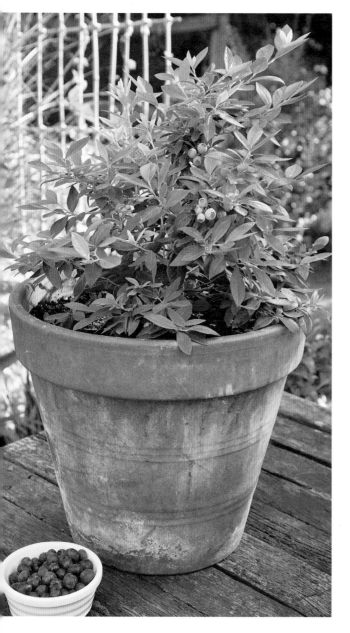

If you're growing just one blueberry, make sure you plant a cultivar that will crop on its own, such as 'Sunshine Blue' or 'Bluecrop' (see p61). If you have the room though, it is well worth growing more than one to guarantee a big crop. Water the blueberry before planting in specialist ericaceous compost. Never use ordinary multipurpose potting compost because it is too alkaline and would cause the plant to die slowly. Mulch with pine needles or bark, which will not upset the acidity of the soil. Give blueberries a sheltered, sunny spot.

Keep plants well watered with rainwater if you can, rather than using tap water (see p60). During the growing season it can be helpful to place a saucer under the pot (see p61).

If you remove the fruit buds as they appear in the first year, you will get a much bigger harvest in the long run. In the second and subsequent years after planting feed blueberry plants with tomato fertilizer once flowering begins.

Remember that berries ripen at different times, which means you need to keep checking and picking regularly so you don't miss any fruit.

Blueberries are a delicious fruit, often hailed as a superfood and expensive to buy in the shops, so they are well worth growing yourself.

Planting your blueberries

What you need

- terra-cotta pot 30cm (12in) or more in diameter;
- drainage material (see p15);
- horticultural grit;
- ericaceous compost;
- young blueberry plant;
- netting.

1 Line the bottom of the pot with drainage material to help water flow away freely. Mix horticultural grit into ericaceous compost – you need about one part grit to two parts compost.

2 Water the blueberry well before planting it at the same level in the compost as it was in its previous pot. The crown of the plant should be just below the surface.

3 Water the plant well and keep the compost moist while the plant is establishing in the pot. Remember to use rainwater for watering because blueberries prefer it to tap water. Then spread mulch around each plant. Water and feed plants regularly (see p60).

4 Protect your berries from greedy birds with netting, making sure it covers the plants completely but is held away from the fruit with canes so that the birds can't peck through it. Use the netting as soon as fruit buds appear since the birds relish these too.

5 Blueberries like warmth; give them as sunny a spot as you can so they can thrive and produce lots of their delicious berries. If the pot is in a hot, sunny spot, pay close attention to watering. Keep picking because the berries ripen at different times.

Currants

Currants are no trouble, look fantastic in full fruit, and have flowers rich in nectar. Red and white currants are quite sour and mainly used for cooking; they can be grown as cordons, fans, and standards. Blackcurrants are vigorous plants, generally grown as bushes, and their fruit has a sweet tartness.

Basic needs

Blackcurrants need a 40cm (16in) pot; red and white currants can go in a 30cm (12in) one. Use loam-based potting compost and grit (see p66).

Growing techniques

1 In the dormant season plant red and white currants at the same level as they were in the pot or ground. Blackcurrants are planted slightly deeper (see p67). Water plants well.

2 Red and white currants tolerate more shade than blackcurrants, although all fruit more quickly and sweetly when grown in the sun.

3 All currants benefit from mulch in spring and watering during dry spells. Feed with a balanced liquid fertilizer in the growing season.

4 Repot every two to three years into a pot of the same size or one only slightly larger. Use fresh potting mix and trim the roots back by one third.

Expert tips

■ Prune in early spring. Blackcurrants need one third of their oldest stems removing at the base. With other currants, cut back to healthy buds, with the aim of maintaining 8–10 well-spaced branches.

■ Lift containers up onto bricks in winter so that excess water can drain freely away.

Problem solving

Birds adore currants so protect your plants (see p67). Blister aphids can disfigure leaf undersides; look out for them in spring. Big bud mites can fatten blackcurrant buds; dispose of infected buds and destroy heavily infested plants.

Harvesting and storage

Currants take longer to ripen than you think – they look ready before they are actually at their best. Cut as bunches and eat fresh, cooked, or make into jellies or jams. They also freeze well.

VARIETIES black: 'Ben Connan', 'Ben Lomond', 'Ben Sarek'; red: 'Jonkheer van Tets', 'Red Lake', 'Stanza'; white: 'Versailles Blanche', 'White Grape'

White currants are slightly smaller and sweeter than red currants but can be used in the same way.

Leave red currants on the bush a little after they look ripe for them to sweeten further.

The longer blackcurrants remain on the bush the sweeter they will be.

Grapes

Even in a small area, it is worth giving grape-growing a go. The vines are attractive in their own right, with their large, handsome leaves, and they can be encouraged to climb over a wall or fence, or grown as a standard if space is really tight. In a sunny site, they will crop readily, and picking your own grapes, whether for eating or for making wine or juice, is a beautiful way to mark the end of the season.

Basic needs

Use loam-based potting compost mixed with grit in a pot 30cm (12in) or more wide (see p69).

Growing techniques

1 Plant from late autumn to late spring (see p68). Water and mulch. Place in a very sunny spot.

2 Once tiny fruit appear give plants a weekly liquid tomato feed.

3 Water well during dry spells, particularly in the first year after planting.

4 Remove all flowers in the first two years; allow only three bunches of grapes on three-year-old plants; then five on four-year-old plants. After this they can flower and fruit freely.

5 Refresh the top 15cm (6in) of potting compost every spring.

Problem solving

Protect fruit against wasps and birds with netting or wrap individual bunches with muslin or old tights. Fungal growth on leaves may be a sign of powdery or downy mildew. The former can spread to stems and fruit (see p34). Grey mould may infect developing bunches of fruit. Ensure that vines are adequately watered to prevent the problem and prune overcrowded shoots.

Harvesting and storage

Grapes are ready when they feel soft, but taste is the better indicator of when to pick. Sometime

Expert tips

- Prune in early winter by cutting all growth back to one or two buds for tight, compact growth.
- Train and thin out young shoots in spring and summer.
- Nip out the leaves around fruit so that the sun can reach the grapes, for ripening.

between late summer and mid-autumn, the fruit should turn sweet and sugary, when the bunches can be cut. Eat dessert grapes straight away or store in the refrigerator for a couple of weeks. Wine grapes can be eaten but are best made into juice or wine.

VARIETIES red wine: 'New York Muscat'; white wine: 'Chardonnay', 'Seyval Blanc'; red dessert: 'Schiava Grossa'; white dessert: 'Muscat of Alexandria', 'Siegerrebe'; dual-purpose: 'Boskoop Glory'

Expose young fruit to sunlight by picking off any leaves that may delay ripening.

Blackcurrant 'superfruits'

These old favourites are bursting with Vitamin C and are expensive in the shops, so are a double delight to grow yourself. They are easy-care, highly productive plants – provided you get to the fruit before the birds! A decorative, glazed container will complement the plant nicely, and it's less porous than terra cotta, so will hold water for longer. Once the fruit have been harvested, pick the leaves to make a lovely tea.

Plant bare-root plants between mid-autumn and winter in a sunny site. Blackcurrants are vigorous growers needing a larger pot than other currants (see p64) and are usually grown as a bush rather than trained in any other way. Plant in loam-based compost mixed 2:1 with horticultural grit to aid drainage. Blackcurrants are planted so that part of the stem is buried, in order to encourage lots of young, vigorous shoots to develop from the base. This will give you a productive, multistemmed bush. Directly after planting cut down some of the shoots; although it will lead to a smaller crop in the first year, the result will be a stronger plant. If planting a container-grown blackcurrant at any other time of year wait until mid-autumn to early spring to do this pruning.

Blackcurrants are particularly hungry and thirsty plants so give them a good mulch in spring and feed and water them well in the growing season.

Bushes do not need pruning the year after planting. Thereafter in early spring cut down up to one third of the old stems almost to soil level – these are a darker colour. This will encourage an open habit and young, fresh growth from the base, which will produce fruit later that season. Repot every two to three years (see opposite).

The leaves of blackcurrants have a distinctive sweet, currantlike scent when crushed, which is a good way to tell one currant from another when they are not in fruit.

Planting a bare-root blackcurrant

What you need

- bare-root blackcurrant plant (see p64);
- bucket of water;
- drainage material (see p15);
- large, ornamental pot 40cm (16in) or more in diameter;
- loam-based potting compost;
- balanced, slow-release fertilizer (see p15);
- secateurs;
- netting.

1 Soak the bare-root plant in a bucket of water as soon as you get it home. Add a layer of drainage material to the base of the pot and then half fill it with potting compost. Mix in the fertilizer to help the roots establish quickly and get your plant off to the best start.

2 Plant your blackcurrant deeply, so that the crown is about 8cm (3½in) below the surface of the compost. This will promote fresh, strong growth from the base. Work the compost around the roots and then fill the rest of the pot with compost, firming it well. Water thoroughly and top up the compost if necessary.

3 After planting cut back some of the stems to 3cm (1¼in) high, using secateurs. Then add a layer of mulch. Water and feed plants regularly.

4 Protect developing fruit from birds by netting plants in early summer. Stretch the netting tautly so the birds cannot peck through it or get caught in it.

5 Harvest modern varieties of blackcurrant by snipping off entire strings. Older types ripen gradually, so fruit should be picked individually.

Grapes on the vine

If you choose your grape variety carefully (see p65) and provide a warm, sunny spot, you should be rewarded with grapes for juicing, wine, or simply eating straight off the vine. In containers, grow the grape as a standard, especially if space is limited. Why not invest in a plant already trained to save you time and bring you closer to your first harvest?

Grapes do well in pots, and in a large one 40cm (16in) wide and deep you could be cropping from the same plant for years. It is advisable however to remove all flowers for the first couple of years (see p65). With the right pruning a grapevine makes an attractive plant – many have magnificent autumn colour too. Ideally container-grown plants should be planted in late spring when growth has already started, while bare-root vines can be planted any time between late autumn and early spring. Grapes like free-draining potting compost, but one that doesn't dry out too quickly, so choose a loam-based one and add some grit. These plants need as much sunshine as you can give them to produce the sugars that make the fruit deliciously sweet, so save your warmest, sunniest spot for them. In front of a sunny wall is perfect. The ideal conditions for a grape however are cool roots, so mulch with large pebbles or include a low-growing plant, such as cranesbill (*Geranium*), to help shield the pot from direct sunlight. Also group the pot with others so they provide shade.

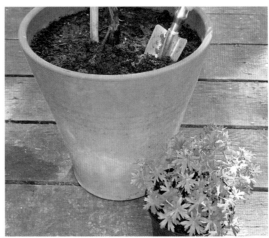

Above: To deflect the sun off the grape's roots include a low-growing plant such as this cranesbill in the pot; it will act as a living mulch and help to keep the pot cool.

Left: Keep on top of watering and feeding and your pot-grown grape should happily produce an abundance of healthy, juicy bunches.

Planting your grape

What you need
- terra-cotta pot 40cm (16in) or more wide and deep;
- drainage material (see p15);
- loam-based potting compost and horticultural grit;
- slow-release fertilizer (see p15); ■ standard grapevine;
- netting.

1 Line the base of the pot with drainage material. Then half fill the pot with the potting compost.

2 Work in a handful of the fertilizer with a trowel. Place the vine, while still in its original pot, on the compost to ensure the plant will be at the same depth as it was previously planted. Adjust the compost depth as appropriate.

3 Remove the vine's pot and place your grape in the centre of the new pot. Fill around the rootball with compost and firm evenly. Then insert the low-growing plant. Water everything in well and mulch.

4 Water your plant regularly in dry summers (see p65). Start feeding your plants once the small bunches of fruit appear, giving them liquid tomato feed each week.

5 Taking care not to nip the developing fruit, remove the leaves around the bunches so the sun can reach them. Protect ripening fruit from the birds with netting. Pick when fruit is sweet and sugary (see p65).

Strawberries

The compact, trailing habit of strawberries makes them ideal for pots or baskets. Also, since the fruits are off the ground, they are easier to look after and to pick, and they are also less vulnerable to slugs and snails. If you grow a combination of different varieties, it is possible to have sweet, fresh strawberries from late spring right through to autumn. Each variety has a short but heavy cropping period of two or three weeks, and they are grouped according to when they fruit – in early, mid-, or late summer. Perpetual strawberries, also known as 'everbearers', are different: they produce small flushes of fruit continuously from early summer to early autumn.

Basic needs

Use any pot, hanging basket (see pp72–73), windowbox, or even grow-bag that is 10cm (4in) or more deep. Six plants will grow well in a basket 35cm (14in) wide; four or five in a grow-bag, windowbox, or pot 20cm (8in) wide. Don't be tempted to grow too many in one pot. Fill each container with good-quality, multipurpose potting compost.

Take care to plant young runners at the correct depth, with the crown level with the soil.

Growing techniques

1 In late summer or early autumn plant strawberries so they have time to get their roots settled before the cold weather sets in. You can also plant in early spring but you will not get a big crop that first year. Make sure the crown is level with the soil surface. If strawberries are planted too deeply they rot; if too high they dry out and die. After planting water well.

2 Give plants a sheltered, sunny spot.

3 Water well and apply a balanced liquid fertilizer after planting to help plants establish. Strawberries are shallow-rooting and dry out quickly, so water little and often to keep the soil moist but without waterlogging it.

Expert tips

- Grow only certified, virus-free varieties purchased from reliable suppliers.
- Covering plants with a cloche or fleece in early spring will encourage flowering, and so fruiting, a week earlier than normal. Remove the cover during the day to help visiting insects pollinate flowers.
- If growing on a windy site or you simply want to ensure a decent crop, pollinate flowers yourself with a small brush.
- Cut off runners, unless you want to propagate new plants, to keep energy focused on flower and fruit production.
- After cropping remove all the old leaves, stems, and runners, as well as straw. Then feed plants with a balanced liquid fertilizer.
- Replace plants after three or four years, when their cropping potential declines.
- Strawberries are easy plants to propagate – allow runners to root and then transplant into individual pots.
- Alpine strawberries, which are smaller than other types, also do brilliantly in pots. They are perpetual strawberries, fruiting right up to the frosts.

A terra-cotta, purpose-made strawberry pot is a handy and fun way to grow a crop of strawberries in a small space.

Harvest strawberries as soon as they are ripe, preferably on a hot, sunny day when the warmth will enhance their flavour.

4 Mulch with straw to conserve water and keep fruit clean and dry.

5 Regular feeding is essential for container-grown strawberries, so give liquid tomato fertilizer every week or so when these plants are flowering and fruiting.

Problem solving

In damp conditions grey mould can be a big problem so always water from below and ensure good air circulation around plants. Birds can be a nuisance too; drape pots with netting. Protect plants against slugs and snails (see p32).

Harvesting and storage

Strawberries are ready for picking when they are a luscious, bright red all over. Harvest them at the warmest time of day for sweet, fragrant fruit. Pick just before eating as strawberries do not keep well. Some varieties such as 'Totem' freeze well, and all can be made into jams.

VARIETIES early: 'Hapil', 'Honeoye', 'Korona'; midsummer: 'Alice', 'Cambridge Favourite', 'Pegasus', 'Totem'; late: 'Florence', 'Rhapsody', 'Symphony'; perpetual: 'Aromel', Mara des Bois', 'Viva Rosa'

Growing strawberries in holes cut into grow-bags saves you having to worry about mulching with straw or plastic.

Strawberry basket

There is something very special about these delicious and gloriously perfumed fruit, and by having your own crop you can pick strawberries when they are at their absolute peak. Fruit grown in a hanging basket will be well away from pesky slugs, and a basket is also a small area to net against birds, which can peck at the crop. As you can grow only a few plants at the top of each basket, give it an added dash by lining it with a pretty oilcloth.

Grow six plants in a 35cm (14in) hanging basket. Although you can use fewer plants in a smaller container (see p70), don't be tempted to use too many plants because overcrowding can cause fungal disease. Buy strawberries as young, potted plants or bare-root runners and plant in late summer to early autumn or spring. To encourage roots to establish and to get a bigger harvest the following year, pinch out the flowers of spring-planted strawberries in the first year.

Keep strawberries well watered – this probably means watering most days during the growing season (see p70). Fill the pot in the centre of the basket (see step 3, right), rather than watering the soil directly. As soon as flowers appear, feed with liquid tomato fertilizer every 7–10 days. At the end of the season give plants a tidy-up, clearing away old leaves, stems, and fruit as well as the straw mulch. This will help expose the crowns to the cold over the winter, which will induce the necessary dormant period for the production of new crowns the following year.

Above: Bees love strawberry flowers and they will buzz around them, pollinating as they go. They dislike windy spots so make sure your basket is sheltered.

Left: For the sweetest, most fragrant fruit, pick during the warmest time of day. Hold the stem and break or cut it off; do not pull the strawberries since they bruise very readily.

Planting your hanging basket

What you need

- hanging basket and liner;
- piece of oilcloth large enough to line the basket;
- marker pen and scissors;
- multipurpose compost;
- 6 x strawberry plants;
- small plastic pot;
- straw or fibre mat.

1 Using the basket liner as a template, draw the liner shape onto the oilcloth with the pen. Then cut out the circular shape marked on the oilcloth.

2 Place the oilcloth in the basket, making sure it is evenly spaced all around the edge. Then puncture some holes in the oilcloth with scissors. Add the liner and fill the basket two thirds full with multipurpose potting compost.

3 Sink a small pot with drainage holes in the centre of the basket – this will help you to water evenly. Then space the strawberry plants evenly around the edge of the basket. Before you water well, add more compost to fill in. Water and feed plants regularly.

4 Once fruit appears, mulch with straw or fibre mat to keep the strawberries away from damp soil. This will stop them rotting and help to conserve moisture. Strawberries hate their roots sitting in damp soil so water them little and often.

5 Pick fruit as soon as it is ripe – strawberries should be a deep, even red all over. Check plants regularly so you don't miss any. Overripe fruit will soon start to break down and rot so it must be discarded immediately before it becomes diseased.

Vegetables

Tomatoes

All tomatoes are ideal for growing in containers. There are three types: the tall cordons, which need staking and pinching out as they grow (see p80); the bush types, which require less maintenance; and trailing tomatoes, which are excellent in hanging baskets (see p78). You can buy young plants in spring, but if you grow your own you'll have a wider choice of good container varieties.

Basic needs

Grow in containers 30–45cm (12–18in) deep filled with loam-based potting compost, or try using grow-bags.

When potting on ensure the tomato stem is buried right up to its first leaves, to encourage further roots from the stem.

You can help flowers set and turn to fruit either by misting them with water or by tapping the flowers.

Growing techniques

1 In early spring place four or five seeds on top of the moist seed compost in a small pot and cover it with cling film to keep humidity levels high.

2 Place the pot on a warm, sunny windowsill. Seeds should germinate within two weeks.

3 Prick out the seedlings into individual pots.

4 Pot them on into larger pots a few weeks later. Once the weather is warm enough and they are big enough to go outside into their final pots, plant one tomato per pot (two per grow-bag) right up to its first leaves. This will help anchor the plant in the pot.

5 In early summer gradually harden off the plants, acclimatizing them to the outdoors over a couple of weeks, before leaving them in direct sun or bright, filtered light outdoors by midsummer.

6 Stake cordon tomatoes as they grow, using canes and twine. You should have only one main stem so pinch out any sideshoots that form in the leaf joints (see p81). Once five trusses have

Expert tips

- Water plants so that the soil is always moist but do not overdo it. Too much water can lead to disease and can cause nutrients to leach out of the soil as well as reduced flavour in fruit.

- Tomatoes are ripe when they are all one colour. Any stragglers still on the plant at the end of summer will not redden before the frosts so bring them indoors to ripen.

- Help your tomatoes by growing companions plants nearby: it is said marigolds keep away whitefly and encourage bees for pollination; borage deters tomato hornworm; and basil makes the flavour of your tomatoes even better.

Carrots and tomatoes are believed to be beneficial companion plants when grown together.

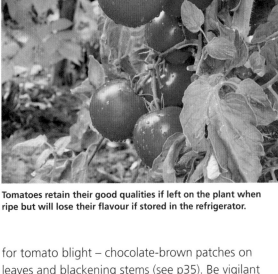

Tomatoes retain their good qualities if left on the plant when ripe but will lose their flavour if stored in the refrigerator.

developed pinch out the top of the plant two leaves above the last truss. This will ensure all your tomatoes have time to ripen before the frosts. Bush and trailing tomatoes are left to grow naturally; they do not need any staking, support, or pinching out.

7 Water plants regularly and feed once a week with liquid tomato fertilizer after the first flowers have developed.

Problem solving

Most problems can be kept at bay with consistent watering and feeding. Irregular watering will cause fruit to split, although these are still perfectly edible. Erratic watering combined with a lack of calcium in the soil can lead to blossom end rot, which makes the bottom of tomatoes turn a leathery black. In wet summers look out

for tomato blight – chocolate-brown patches on leaves and blackening stems (see p35). Be vigilant and act quickly if these symptoms appear. At the first signs of tomato blight it is best to pick all your fruit, letting it ripen indoors.

Harvesting and storage

Ripe tomatoes will happily remain on the plant for a couple of weeks, which is handy as they taste best when eaten fresh. They will keep at room temperature for four or five days and can be frozen as purée or ready-made sauces. Tomatoes can also be bottled or dried as well as made into pickles and chutneys.

VARIETIES bush: 'Legend', Tornado'; cordon: 'Gardener's Delight', 'Shirley', 'Sungold'; trailing: 'Hundreds and Thousands', 'Tumbler'

Cherry tomato basket

If you are running out of room, hanging baskets are the answer. They make the most of your vertical space, look fantastic, and can be really productive. Bush and trailing tomatoes have been specially bred to grow in small pots and baskets, and with their spreading habit will spill over and down the sides. They produce masses of sweet, aromatic fruit too. These are brilliantly low-maintenance types and can be left to get on with it.

For your hanging basket choose a coir or sisal liner rather than the more traditional sphagnum moss one, and add a circle of plastic, cut from an old compost bag, to the base to aid water retention. Tomatoes are hungry and thirsty plants so one will be enough for a standard basket, 35cm (14in) wide. When planting, sit the basket in a large plant pot to keep it stable if it is wobbling. Multipurpose potting compost is best in baskets as loam-based compost is too

heavy when wet. To help retain moisture during a dry summer or the times when you cannot be around to water, mix water-retaining gel into the compost before you plant. Keep the compost moist (see p76), which may well mean watering every day, and as soon as flowers appear start feeding your tomato plants weekly.

Opposite: A tomato in a hanging basket can be just as eye-catching as one filled with summer flowers. If possible hang it by the kitchen door for easy pickings.

Planting your tomato basket

What you need
■ hanging basket; ■ coir or sisal liner; ■ circle of plastic, cut from an old compost bag; ■ multipurpose potting compost; ■ water-retaining gel; ■ slow-release fertilizer (optional); ■ bush type tomato (see p77).

1 Place the liner in the hanging basket, keeping it flush at the edges. Line the bottom with some plastic from an old compost bag. Fill about two thirds of the basket with potting compost.

2 Add some water-retaining gel, according to the manufacturer's instructions, and mix it into the compost well. You can also add some slow-release fertilizer (see p15) at this stage if you wish.

3 Plant the tomato in the centre of the basket, as deep as its first true leaves, and fill in with compost, firming as you go. Leave a gap between the compost and the top of the basket to make watering easier. Water well after planting.

4 As soon as the first yellow flowers begin to form, give your plant liquid tomato fertilizer every week. (Our plant was already in flower so we fed it straight after planting.) Keep the compost moist by watering these thirsty plants very regularly.

5 Tomatoes are always at their most delicious when eaten fresh and warmed by the sunshine. Try to pick them straight from the vine whenever possible.

Long Tom tomato

The taste of a home-grown tomato fresh from the vine is unbeatable – a rich, sweet tang that's missing from even the best shop-bought fruit, and for this reason alone they are one of the most popular crops to grow. Give them a helping hand and ensure the best harvest possible by growing them with companions such as French marigolds (*Tagetes patula*) and basil. Some people believe basil deters whitefly and even intensifies the flavour of the fruit, while marigolds will encourage pollinating bees.

There are hundreds of different varieties of tomato available, from the tender cherry to burly beefsteaks (see p77), and all of them can be started from seed indoors in early spring, by sowing them in small pots and placing them on a warm, sunny windowsill (see p76). They will need potting on into larger pots after about seven weeks and can be planted outside in early summer. Alternatively you can buy young plants from the garden centre or by mail order. Harden off young plants for a few days before planting out and then give them the warmest, sunniest spot in your garden. Grow only one plant per container as tomatoes are hungry, thirsty plants. Their compost mustn't dry out, which will mean watering every day in hot weather.

Make sure you know which tomato type you are growing, as cordon tomatoes need to be tied into stakes, and their sideshoots pinched out. Give plants at least a weekly liquid tomato feed once the flowers appear. Pick the marigold flowers.

Above: Harvest the tomatoes when they are a gorgeous red all over and eat them straight away. They will ripen gradually up the vine as you continue cropping.

Left: Keeping on top of regular tasks such as pinching out sideshoots and tying the tomato to its cane will result in a tall, slender plant on a single stem.

Planting your long Tom tomato

What you need

- small pots, multipurpose compost, cordon tomato seed, and cling film, if sowing;
- terra-cotta long Tom pot;
- drainage material (see p15);
- loam-based potting compost;
- bamboo cane and twine;
- 3 x basil, 3 x marigold.

1 Sow four or five seeds in a small pot of moist multipurpose compost in early spring, cover with cling film, and place on a sunny windowsill. Keep the compost moist. Pot on plants into individual pots (see p76). Grow on until it is warm enough for the plants to go outside.

2 In early summer line the base of the long Tom with drainage material. Then half fill it with loam-based potting compost. Plant one tomato deeply in the centre of the pot, burying it up to its first set of healthy leaves (see p76). Top up the compost and water the plant well.

3 Stake the tomato plant, tying it to the cane with twine. Then insert the basil and marigold plants around the tomato, and water the plants again and mulch. (If you prefer, you could plant up your other seed-raised tomato plants similarly.)

4 Keep tying the tomato into the cane as it develops. Feed and water plants regularly. Nip out the growing points of the basil to make stockier plants and discourage flowering. Harvest the basil leaves regularly.

5 Pinch out any sideshoot that grows in a leaf joint between the main stem and a side branch. Once the tomato has grown five trusses, pinch out the top of the plant two leaves above the last truss. Pick the tomatoes as they mature.

Aubergines

With their exotic, purple flowers, plump, glossy fruit, and beautiful, downy leaves, aubergines make a handsome sight. An array of colours and sizes is available, but the fruit all have the same delicious, creamy taste.

Basic needs

Grow in a pot 30cm (12in) in diameter filled with good-quality, multipurpose potting compost, for a single plant. Dwarf varieties will fit into something a little smaller. Three plants will grow happily in a grow-bag.

Growing techniques

1 Aubergines need long, hot summers, so if growing in cool-temperate areas choose varieties with small, slender fruit, which need less ripening (see p84). Grow them from young plants to give them sufficient time to develop and ripen; grafted plants may give you even more of a head-start.

2 If growing from seed, sow in early spring and place the pot on a warm, light windowsill, at 20°C (68°F). Do not let the compost dry out.

3 When big enough to handle, prick seedlings out into individual pots. They can be planted out into their final pots when frosts have definitely

Ripe, glossy aubergines such as this one are delicious when sliced and roasted in olive oil over a barbecue in summer.

passed, but harden them off for a few days first.

4 Grow aubergine in your hottest, sunniest spot, preferably against a warm wall.

5 Once first fruit appears, feed every two weeks with liquid tomato fertilizer.

Expert tips

- Once plants reach 30cm (12in) pinch out the main tip to encourage sideshoots.
- Stake larger plants.
- Help fruiting by tapping flowers to release pollen, rubbing them with a small paint brush, or misting with water.
- Remove petals sticking to fruit to prevent grey mould.
- Nip off lower leaves as the fruit swells to improve air flow.

Problem solving

Mist foliage daily to deter red spider mite. Rub aphids off by hand whenever they are seen (see p34). Remove growth infected by grey mould at once. Regular watering prevents blossom end rot.

Harvesting and storage

Pick fruit when fully coloured and glossy. It will keep for a couple of weeks in the refrigerator. Aubergine can be pickled or frozen in sauces.

VARIETIES 'Amethyst', 'Baby Belle', 'Baby Rosanna', 'Calliope', 'Fairy Tale', 'Falcon', 'Galine', 'Mohican', 'Moneymaker', 'Slim Jim'

Peppers & chillies

Both sweet and chilli peppers are definitely worth growing, but they do need a long, sunny season. There's a world of difference between shop-bought and home-grown peppers so give different shapes and colours a try. Why not give yourself a head-start by growing on young plants, especially grafted ones – it will make a successful harvest much more likely.

Basic needs

Grow in a container 30cm (12in) in diameter with good drainage and filled with multipurpose potting compost, one for each plant. Three plants will fit in a grow-bag. Very compact varieties will also grow in a hanging basket.

Growing techniques

1 Grow from young plants (see p86), or sow indoors from late winter to mid-spring (see p87).

2 Keep well watered and be patient – seeds can be slow to germinate.

3 Place the pot in a hot, sunny spot – the base of a warm wall is ideal (see p86) or grow peppers under glass.

4 Water regularly in dry weather, and when flowering apply a balanced liquid fertilizer.

Problem solving

Usually trouble-free.

Harvesting and storage

Although peppers and chillies come in a range of colours, they generally mature from green through to red. Pick fruit at whichever stage of colour you prefer (see p87). Eat fresh, slow-dry them in the oven, or hang up to air dry (see p86).

VARIETIES chillies: 'Apache', 'Chenzo', 'Fiesta', 'Filius Blue', 'Gusto Purple', 'Hungarian Hot Wax'; sweet peppers: 'Ace', 'Friggitello', 'Gourmet', 'Marconi Rosso', 'Mohawk', 'Redskin', 'Roberta'

Pinch out the growing tips of plants when they have reached 20cm (8in), or just above the fifth set of leaves. This will encourage bushy growth (see above) and lots more fruit.

Some chillies should be harvested when they are still green to encourage the plant to fruit further. The other fruits can then be left to redden at the end of the season.

Expert tips

- Pinch out growing tips to encourage bushy growth.

- Assist pollination by brushing flower to flower with a paint brush.

- Get a head-start by overwintering plants in a warm glasshouse or conservatory. Prune them well and water sparingly.

Shiny, black aubergines

Aubergines are an expensive vegetable in the shops and don't taste a patch on the flavoursome smoothness of ones you can grow yourself. Large pots, which are needed for a good crop, can be expensive, so adapt other containers such as black, plastic storage crates for a good, cheap alternative. They also set off the polished, black fruit beautifully.

Aubergines need a really long, hot growing season so, if there is one crop you are going to grow from a young plant bought at the garden centre rather than grow it from seed, this is it. Don't worry about cheating – you need all the help you can get with aubergines, especially if you are growing it in a cool-temperate area. Get plants as soon as they appear on the shelves and pot them on, growing them on a bright, warm windowsill until the weather is warm enough for them to go in their crates outside.

Give aubergine plants your brightest, hottest spot. Once they reach 20–30cm (8–12in), pinch out the growing tips (see opposite) to promote bushy growth. As soon as flowering begins, give plants a weekly feed with liquid tomato fertilizer and brush the flowers to assist pollination (see p82). Larger fruiting varieties may need staking with a cane to keep them upright.

Opposite: Harvest fruit when they are still a shiny, glossy indigo-black or they will quickly turn bitter.

Planting your aubergine crate

What you need
- black plastic storage crate;
- screwdriver or drill;
- drainage material (see p15);
- multipurpose potting compost;
- 2 x aubergine plants (see p82).

1 Any container that is not specifically a plant pot will always need holes punched or drilled into the base if it does not already have them. Then add a layer of drainage material and fill two thirds of the crate with the compost.

2 Position plants on the compost surface while still in their pots to establish the correct planting depth – this should be the same as it is in each pot. Then remove each plant from its pot and plant, adding more compost to fill. Water in well, then mulch.

3 Aubergines are large, hungry, thirsty plants and particularly when grown in pots, so water regularly, never letting them dry out and protect them from slugs and snails (see p32). Give them a liquid tomato feed once a week.

4 When each plant reaches 20–30cm (8–12in) high nip out its growing tip with your fingertips to encourage fresh, bushy growth and quicker, heavier, earlier fruiting.

5 Fruit is best picked when young and shiny, otherwise it has a tendency to turn woolly inside and develop masses of bitter-tasting seeds. Early cropping also encourages further ripening.

Chilli hotpots

The spicy kick of a chilli can transform so many dishes, and they pack quite a punch in the garden too. It is well worth giving them a decent pot, such as these classic terra-cotta planters, rather than settling for plastic ones. Growers get quite fanatical about chillies, and there are now hundreds of varieties to choose from, so take your pick. Grow a collection and you will have enough to see you well into the new year.

Chillies can be sown any time from late winter until the end of spring, but the earlier you sow the longer the plants have to ripen. Late winter is the ideal time. Alternatively you can buy young plants, which are readily available from garden centres and by mail order (see p83). However such sources do not offer the same variety of colour and shape that you get from seed nurseries. Cover freshly sown seed with cling film to keep humidity levels up and promote germination, and keep the compost moist. When planting outside give plants a sheltered, sunny spot – the hotter the better – because they need a long, warm summer to ripen. Pinching out the growing tips will promote bushier growth and therefore more fruit (see p83). Large, heavily laden plants may well need help by tying them onto two or more supporting canes. Feed with tomato fertilizer once a week when the flowers appear, and give the bees a hand by pollinating flowers yourself with a small brush or cotton bud. Leaving the first set of fruit on the plant to mature to red will result in far fewer chillies, so harvest the first fruit when they are green and then you'll get fruit right through into autumn.

Above: An attractive way of drying peppers is to thread string or cotton through each fruit and hang in the warm.

Left: The hotter the chilli, such as the habaneros (in the right-hand pot), the longer they can take to ripen, which is well worth bearing in mind in cool-temperate areas.

Sowing your chilli seeds

What you need

- small pots for sowing and growing on; ■ multipurpose compost; ■ chilli seeds – 3 different varieties (see p83); ■ cling film; ■ terra-cotta pots at least 30cm (12in) wide; ■ bamboo canes and twine; ■ drainage material (see p15).

1 Fill 7cm (2¹⁄₂in) pots with the potting compost, firming it down gently to remove any air holes. Water the compost to moisten it before sowing. Sow two seeds per pot. Cover the seed by sprinkling lightly with more compost.

2 Water again gently and cover the pots with cling film. Place on a warm, light windowsill. Remove the cling film after germination. When seedlings sprout a second set of leaves, nip out the weaker seedling to leave one healthy plant in each pot. Keep the compost moist.

3 When the young plants reach about 12cm (5in) high, pot them on into larger pots. Water well. Once they reach 20cm (8in) high, tie each plant to a small bamboo cane for support. Protect plants from attack by slugs and snails (see p32).

4 As soon as the weather is warm enough and all frosts have passed, the plants can go out into final pots. Cover each base with a good layer of drainage material, then fill with compost and plant up. Stake each plant. Initially cover with a cloche in cool-temperate areas.

5 Water and feed plants regularly. Rather than leave the first fruit to turn red, snip off the first chillies when they are still green. You will then get more fruit, and these can then be left on the plant to ripen fully to a bright, glossy red.

Courgettes

Courgettes are one of the quickest, easiest, and most productive crops, and are definitely worth growing considering how much they cost in the shops. But do not overdo it – you only need one or two plants to keep you in an abundance of courgettes all summer long. Despite taking up lots of room in the veg plot, they are very happy in large pots, especially if you choose a compact variety.

Basic needs

Courgettes are hungry, thirsty plants so use a large container, 60cm (2ft) wide, or grow-bag. Mix potting compost with well-rotted manure and a sprinkle of general-purpose fertilizer.

Growing techniques

1 Sow seed in late spring, or grow from shop-bought plants in early summer. Set 2–3 seeds on their sides in the pot or grow-bag and place in a warm, sunny spot.

2 Thin to leave one strong seedling per pot.

3 Keep potting compost moist, particularly once the fruit starts to swell. Water around plants rather than over them, to prevent rotting.

4 Once fruit appears feed every couple of weeks with a tomato or balanced liquid fertilizer.

Problem solving

Protect pots against slugs (see p32). Prevent powdery mildew by keeping plants well watered, particularly during late summer (see p34).

By picking courgettes when they are still young you will promote a large, continuous harvest.

Try harvesting with flowers still attached. These can be fried whole or tossed into salads.

Expert tips

- Since courgette seeds are large, flat, and have a tendency to rot, always sow them on their narrow sides.
- Sinking a small plant pot into the compost next to the plant and watering into it will ensure the water goes down to the plant's roots where it is needed, and doesn't sit around the crown causing rot.

Harvesting and storage

Harvest from midsummer to mid-autumn when courgettes are about 10cm (4in) long. Keep picking regularly so they do not get too big. Eat fresh; chop, blanch, and freeze; or make into jams or plckles. Flowers are also lovely in salads or when stuffed and fried.

VARIETIES bush: 'Bambino', 'Jemmer', 'Romanesco', 'Tristan', 'Venus'; climbing: 'Black Forest', 'Tondo Chairo di Nizza', 'Tromboncino'

Cucumbers

Cucumbers are gratifyingly easy to grow, asking only for sun and something to climb up before rewarding you with heaps of fruit and beautiful, bright flowers. The longer, smooth-skinned varieties need a warm, humid environment, while smaller, prickly 'ridge' cucumbers grow very happily in cool-temperate climates – just choose a variety to suit your conditions.

Basic needs
Grow individually in any pot, tub, trough, or grow-bag provided it is 25cm (10in) in diameter and 20cm (8in) deep. Fill the container with loam-based potting compost.

Growing techniques
1 In mid-spring sow seed in warm conditions, a minimum temperature 20°C (68°F), or buy young plants in late spring. Sow the seeds on their sides to prevent rotting, and cover (see p91).

2 Grow in a warm, sheltered site or under glass, and mulch plants to conserve moisture.

3 Keep the potting compost moist, watering

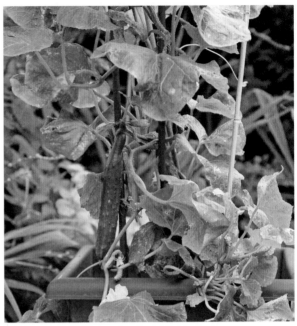

Cucumbers are attractive, exotic-looking plants with their large, tropical leaves, golden flowers, and prolific fruit.

around plants rather than over them (see p90).

4 Train longer, smooth-skinned varieties up a wigwam, canes, or trellis. Smaller types can be left to trail over the pot.

5 Feed every two weeks with a liquid tomato fertilizer once the fruit starts to develop.

Problem solving
Protect pots against slugs (see p32). Ensure plants are always moist to prevent powdery mildew (see p34); remove affected leaves at once and spray with water to keep conditions humid.

Harvesting and storage
The skin toughens with age so pick cucumbers young. Store in the refrigerator for up to a week.

VARIETIES indoors: 'Bella', 'Femdan', 'Zeina'; outdoors: 'Chinese Slangen', 'Crystal Lemon', 'Marketmore', 'Tokyo Slicer'

Expert tips

- Choose F1 cultivars of smooth-skinned types, as they are all-female plants. Otherwise plants will need their male flowers removed to stop them pollinating the female ones and causing bitter fruit.

- Plants hate root disturbance so either sow cucumbers in their final pots or in biodegradable pots to reduce stress later.

- Place a collar around each plant stem to stop it rotting (see p91).

- Focus energy into fruit production by pinching out the growing tips.

Climbing cucumber

A single cucumber in a large pot will keep you in crisp, juicy fruit all summer long. In fact you may have trouble keeping up with these prolific plants. Despite their striking, exotic looks they are surprisingly easy to grow – just give them a warm spot, plenty of food and water, and keep on picking!

Make sure you have chosen the right cucumber to grow outdoors, as indoor types will not cope in the cooler conditions outdoors (see p89). Cucumbers hate having their roots disturbed; therefore, if growing from seed, sow into biodegradable pots – of coir, for example – and you can plant them out, pot and all. Harden plants off gradually over a week or so, before planting them outside in a warm, sunny, sheltered place. Alternatively sow seed directly outside at the beginning of summer and cover with a cloche or large glass jar, or grow them under glass.

Pinch out the growing tip once seven leaves have developed, and then train the sideshoots up and around an obelisk, pinching out flowerless shoots after five leaves. Growing cucumbers up such a support saves space. You can however also let cucumbers trail over the side of the pot and along the ground. Being almost all water, cucumbers are very thirsty plants, particularly in pots, so keep them well watered. Unfortunately they are very susceptible to rot, so water around the plant rather than drenching the leaves and stems. Every two weeks give them liquid tomato fertilizer once the fruit starts to appear.

A cucumber plant dripping with fruit can be heavy, so ensure that it is securely tied to its support and that the support is well embedded in the container.

Sowing your cucumber seed

What you need
- small biodegradable pots;
- multipurpose potting compost; ■ cucumber seeds (see p89); ■ cling film; ■ pot at least 30cm (12in) wide and deep; ■ drainage material (see p15); ■ collar made from old plastic pot; ■ obelisk; ■ twine.

1 Sow two seeds on their sides in each biodegradable pot filled with compost. Cover with cling film and place on a warm, bright windowsill. Remove the cling film after germination. Snip out the weakest seedling. As the plant grows, pot it on.

2 When ready, plant the cucumber just off-centre in the final pot, filled with compost and a layer of drainage. Make sure the top of the rootball is level with the compost surface. To stop the stem rotting make a collar by cutting away the base of an old plastic pot.

3 Slip the collar of the old plastic pot around the stem of the cucumber plant. Water well and mulch. Place an obelisk in the middle of the pot to act as support for your plant. Protect young plants from slugs and snails (see p32).

4 Help the plant up its support by regularly tying stems to the obelisk with garden twine. Keep plants well watered (see p89) and feed them regularly. Pinch out tendrils so the plant focuses its energy on flower and fruit production.

5 Harvest cucumbers at any size, by cutting each off with a sharp knife. If fruit is left to get too big it will also become less tasty and lose its texture.

Pumpkins & squash

It is difficult to go wrong with squash and pumpkins. They are easy to grow, look amazing, and keep well, so you can still enjoy them long after the plants have died. Available in an incredible range of shapes, sizes, and colours, they can climb or trail. There are also compact, bushy types.

Basic needs
Grow one plant per 45cm (18in) pot and fill it with a mix of three parts loam-based potting compost to one part well-rotted manure or garden compost. A couple of plants will fit in a grow-bag.

Growing techniques
1 Sow outside in late spring or early summer, two seeds per pot, 2.5cm (1in) deep.

Expert tips

- Sow seeds upright, on their narrow sides, to prevent rotting.
- Leave heavier fruiting pumpkins to trail – they are difficult to support vertically.
- If weather turns wet keep fruit off damp surfaces by placing them on old tiles.

2 Cover the pot with a cloche for as long as you can after germination. Thin out, leaving the strongest seedling.

3 Alternatively plant out young plants when frosts have passed. Water well.

4 Keep the soil moist, watering around the plant rather than onto it. Mulch to conserve moisture.

5 Support trailing squash with a wigwam.

6 As soon as the fruit starts to swell give plants a balanced liquid feed every couple of weeks.

Problem solving
Protect plants, especially when young, from slugs and snails (see p32).

Harvesting and storage
Leave fruit to ripen on the plant for as long as you can and then cut with a short stem, before the frost. Listen for a hollow sound when you tap the fruit; this indicates that it is ripe. Store in a cool, dry place where the fruit will keep for several months. Seeds of pumpkins and squash are delicious – and nutritious too.

VARIETIES pumpkin: 'Baby Bear'; squash: 'Butterbush', 'Cobnut', 'Early Butternut', 'Harrier', 'Hawk', 'Hunter', 'Uchiki Kuri'

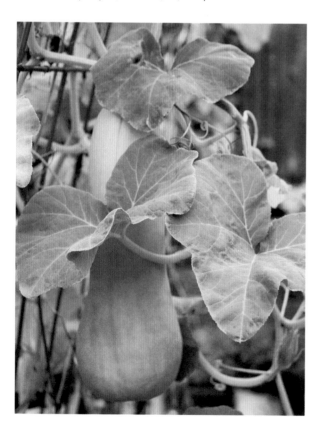

Encouraging squash or pumpkins to climb up a wigwam, obelisk, or canes helps to keep the ripening fruit (such as this butternut squash) off damp soil in autumn.

Sweet potatoes

Actually a vine and not related to traditional potatoes at all, sweet potatoes are a great crop for pots. These rambling, clambering plants are in the soil a long time, but a pot takes up much less space and contains them nicely. Once planted sweet potato plants can be pretty much left to get on with it while you wait for the fun of harvesting. Traditionally a warm-climate crop, hardier cultivars are now available for cool-temperate areas.

Basic needs
Grow in a large container, 60cm (24in) wide, with good drainage holes filled with a 50:50 mix of sand and multipurpose potting compost. A large, black, plastic tub is good in cool-temperate climates because it absorbs heat.

Growing techniques
1 Grow as unrooted cuttings – slips – or small plugs. Choose the latter in cool-temperate areas.

2 Pot slips into individual small pots. Water and place on a sunny windowsill until well rooted.

3 Harden off before planting out into their final pots (see p95). Set them in a warm, sunny place.

4 In cool-temperate climates cover plants with cloches (see p95) or fleece for as long as you can.

5 Feed every other week with a balanced liquid fertilizer. Water well in dry spells.

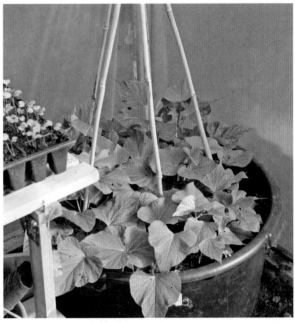

For a better crop with larger tubers give sweet potatoes some support to climb, such as a wigwam of bamboo canes.

Expert tips

- Train plants up a wigwam placed over the centre of the pot, helping them on with some soft twine.
- Sweet potatoes will rot if frozen so lift tubers if frost threatens late in the season.

In a good summer sweet potatoes will reward you with their gorgeous blooms.

Problem solving
Slugs love the leaves so go on regular collecting missions at night and destroy them (see p32).

Harvesting and storage
Tubers can take up to five months to mature and are ready when the leaves turn yellow and start to die back (see p95). Skins need to harden so leave tubers somewhere warm to cure for a few days before storing in a cool, dark place. Foliage and young shoots are also tasty; pick when you require them.

VARIETIES 'Beauregard', 'Georgia Jet', 'O'Henry', 'T65'

Sweet potato bags

These attractive, scrambling vines can take over a small garden if left unchecked. Therefore they are better grown in deep, purpose-made planters or bags so you can stop them rooting wherever they land. The tubers make a delicious, undemanding crop, and you can also eat the leaves and young shoots of sweet potatoes like spinach – just don't be greedy as too little foliage will reduce your harvest!

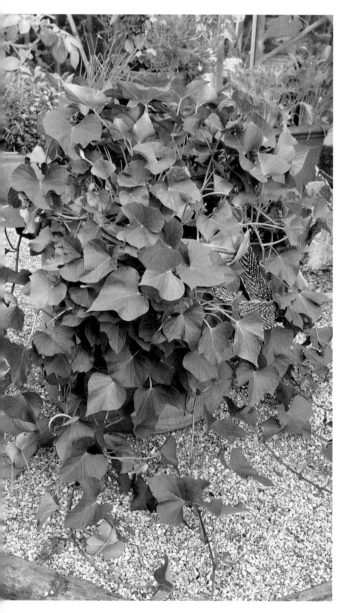

Sweet potatoes are not grown from tubers, like true potatoes, but from slips, which are cuttings, or young plants. Slips need to be grown on before planting in their final container. Therefore if you live in cool-temperate areas and young plants are available, go for these instead of slips because of the short growing season. Plant them straight into your planter. Give sweet potatoes rich, well-drained soil by mixing multipurpose potting compost with sand (see p93). This is a warm-climate crop so it needs heat to grow well and extra protection; use cloches for as long as you can if temperatures are cool.

Sweet potatoes are rampant plants and will take up much less room if you train them up supports. This will also help to stop these tenacious climbers from rooting wherever their leaf nodes touch the soil, giving you a fiddly crop of lots of little tubers, rather than fewer, larger ones. Guide them back onto their canes every few weeks.

Water sweet potatoes regularly as they are thirsty plants, but don't overdo it – they hate sitting in wet soil. Give them a balanced liquid feed every couple of weeks.

To get a head-start next year, take stem cuttings at the end of summer and root them in water. Then pot up and overwinter them in a frost-free spot, ready for planting early next year.

Sweet potatoes are attractive, exotic-looking, scrambling plants, quite unlike traditional potatoes in appearance. Their handsome leaves can also be picked and eaten.

Planting your sweet potatoes

What you need

- sweet potato slips;
- large jar of water;
- tall pots or root trainers;
- multipurpose potting compost;
- horticultural sand;
- potato planter and cloche;
- bamboo canes and twine.

1 Unwrap the potato slips as soon as they arrive. They may look a little wilted and tired, so place them in a jar of water overnight to revive them.

2 The next day insert the slips up to the base of the leaves into a tall pot or root trainer filled with compost mix (see p93). Water well. Grow on under cover for 2–3 weeks, until plants have established decent root systems.

3 Fill your planter with fresh multipurpose compost and sand mix and plant up, spacing plants evenly around the edge. A 60-litre planter (as here) should have space for five plants, while a pot of 50cm (20in) diameter should hold 5–6 plants. Water well.

4 Protect young plants under a cloche for as long as feasible in cool-temperate areas. Feed and water plants regularly. After removing the cover, support each plant by erecting a wigwam of canes over the planter, with one cane for each plant to twine up (see p93).

5 Harvest crops carefully so as not to bruise the tubers and cure their skins by storing them for about 10 days in a humid, airy place. Be sure to collect your crop before the frosts, which will destroy tubers.

Potatoes

Potatoes are a crop that traditionally takes up a lot of room in the ground, but it is surprisingly successful in containers. Although the yield will not be huge, the secret with potatoes is depth, so choose your container carefully and concentrate on growing the delicious, more unusual, new potatoes that are either unavailable in the shops or expensive when they are. New potatoes are usually harvested early too, which means you should avoid the frustrating disappointment of blight.

Basic needs

Potatoes will grow in just about anything that is at least 30cm (12in) wide and deep with good drainage, including purpose-made bags, rubber tub trugs, and even old compost bags. Grow them in multipurpose potting compost.

Harvest potatoes carefully either by upturning bags and pots or by rummaging gently with a small handfork.

Growing techniques

1 Chit potatoes before planting, which means help them to sprout. To do this stand them in egg boxes or on trays in a cool, light place, with the end bearing the most eyes upward (see p98). When shoots are around 2.5cm (1in) long the tubers can be planted out.

2 Depending on type, plant from early spring (see p98). Place the container in a sunny spot, then fill it with 20cm (8in) potting compost and sprinkle in a little fertilizer (see p99). Plant the chitted tubers – two is ample for a container 30cm (12in) in diameter – and cover with 10cm (4in) of potting compost. Then water it.

3 As the plants grow keep covering their shoots and leaves with compost (see p99) until the soil almost reaches the top of the pot.

4 Potatoes need a consistent supply of water for the best harvest, so keep plants well watered, particularly while tubers are starting to develop.

5 Give a liquid feed regularly (see p98).

Problem solving

Your biggest challenge will be avoiding blight, a fungal disease that can wipe out an entire potato crop (see p35). It flourishes in warm, wet weather and usually strikes around late summer, so the best way to beat blight is to grow early varieties, which are out of the ground before it hits. Otherwise be vigilant; at the first sign of its

Chitted potatoes grow well in bags. As the potato plants develop, gradually unroll the bag sides and top up the potting compost until it reaches the top of each bag.

distinctive, chocolate blotching cut leaves down to the ground to stop the blight spreading to the tubers underground. Leave the potatoes in the pot for a couple of weeks to harden their skins and hope you have a crop left. Another, much less significant problem – scab – causes marking on the skins and, although it is mainly a decorative problem and can easily be peeled off, you should not store affected potatoes.

Harvesting and storage

Earlies should be ready when in flower. They are best eaten straight away, so lift only when you need them. You can start to lift maincrops any time after flowering. When the foliage turns yellow, cut it down; then leave potatoes for a week or so to harden their skins. After lifting, dry them in the sun for a few hours. Store in the dark in breathable bags – hessian is perfect.

The later you leave maincrop potatoes the bigger the tubers will get, although the longer you leave them the greater the risk of pest or disease.

VARIETIES first earlies: 'Accent', 'Riviera', 'Winston'; second earlies: 'Charlotte', 'Duke of York', 'Kondor','Pixie'; maincrop: 'Pink Fir Apple', 'Ratte', 'Sarpo'

Bags of potatoes

Potatoes will grow in just about anything as long as the container has enough depth, and these bright, cheery, recycled bags make easy and attractive planters. They are ideal for those who don't have much space or for growers who don't want what space they do have dominated by just one demanding crop.

In addition to recycled bags made from porous fabric, you can also plant chitted seed potatoes in purpose-made planters or use tub trugs, which are easy to drill holes in yourself. Grow from early until late spring for summer crops or plant in late summer for harvests in the winter right up until Christmas. If your space is limited, go for the more flavoursome, new potato varieties so your harvests are really special (see p97). Look for blight-resistant varieties if fungal disease could be a problem.

Place bags in a sunny spot and feed plants every other week with specialized potato fertilizer or a balanced liquid one. When wanting to harvest early potatoes have a gentle feel in the bag first to establish the size of the tubers and, if they are too small, give them another week to develop.

Opposite: Make sure the potatoes are clean and dry before storing. To do this, leave harvested potatoes on the soil for a couple of hours until the soil on them is dry. The tubers will rot if stored when still damp.

Planting your potato sack

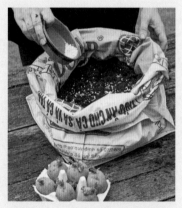

What you need
- 4 x seed potatoes per bag;
- egg box or seed tray;
- potato planter, recycled bag, or tub trug;
- multipurpose potting compost;
- specialized potato fertilizer.

1 Get your seed potatoes started by chitting them, that is, stand them in old egg boxes or seed trays in a cool, light place. Most of the buds, or chits, will be on one end, usually called the rose end, so make sure these are all facing upward.

2 In late spring or early summer plant out the chitted potatoes. Their shoots will be 1–2.5cm (1/2–1in) long. Add 20cm (8in) potting compost to the bottom of the bag and mix in a scoop of potato fertilizer.

3 Place the chitted potatoes, rose ends up, in the compost. Then cover them with 10–20cm (4–8in) more compost. Water the compost well. Fertilize them every two weeks.

4 As they grow keep adding compost to the bag at regular intervals, covering the shoots and leaves each time. Continue this earthing up until the compost is about 5cm (2in) from the top of the bag.

5 Water the bags well in dry weather, particularly when the plants are flowering. Early potatoes are ready to harvest when in flower; maincrops are harvested after the foliage has started to fade (see p97).

Beetroot

Delicious when young and tender, beetroot is a healthy, versatile crop that gives you an extra harvest since the spinachlike leaves are edible too. It works well in a container, sown closely together for lots of small, sweet roots. Beetroot is also great as a catch crop, being sown and harvested while waiting for other crops to come up (see p102). Sow little and often for a regular supply.

Basic needs

Grow in a large container, 30–40cm (12–16in) in diameter, filled with loam-based or multipurpose potting compost. A large container will help to hold in more moisture, which beetroot likes.

Growing techniques

1 Sow seed from mid-spring to midsummer, making regular sowings every couple of weeks.

2 Thin out seedlings regularly so they have plenty of room in which to develop.

3 Keep plants well watered, especially as the roots start to swell, and feed regularly.

Expert tips

■ Don't be tempted to sow too early. Germination can be erratic – wait until mid-spring before starting to do so.

■ Remove the leaves by twisting, rather than cutting them, to stop bleeding (see p102).

Problem solving

Choose bolt-resistant varieties if sowing early – cooler weather can cause early flowering. To stop plants running to seed keep the potting compost moist. Net plants if birds are bothersome.

Harvesting and storage

Lift when roots are the size of a golf ball and eat fresh, grated raw, or cooked, or you can pickle and store beets. Eat leaves as chard (see p113).

VARIETIES 'Action', 'Boltardy', 'Burpee's Golden', 'Cylindra', 'Moneta', 'Monodet', 'Pablo', 'Pronto', 'Red Ace', 'Solo'

The more space you give beetroot when you thin out young seedlings the larger the roots you will get.

Beetroot is one of the few crops that delivers a truly delicious double harvest – its leaves and roots are edible.

Carrots

Home-grown carrots are loaded with sweetness and they work brilliantly in pots, and you'll avoid any problems you might otherwise suffer from heavy or stony soil in open ground. You'll also be able to bamboozle carrot fly, by growing plants above the height at which it can fly. Finally the many short-rooted, speedy varieties mean you can dot carrots among other veg or sow a crop while you are waiting for something else to grow.

Basic needs

Grow in any container, tub, or trough 20cm (8in) or more deep. Use multipurpose potting compost over a base layer of grit, to give carrots the light, well-drained medium that they love.

Growing techniques

1 For main-season crops sow seed from mid-spring to midsummer (see p105).

2 Sow thinly to reduce the amount of thinning needed later – mixing the tiny seed with sand helps and also provides extra drainage.

3 Sow short, successional rows every few weeks for a constant supply of carrots.

4 Although drought resistant, keep the plants watered to prevent woody roots. Feed regularly.

Problem solving

Carrot fly are drawn to the smell of crushed,

Unless harvesting a whole crop of carrots at once, avoid lifting them during the day, when carrot fly are around. Instead, wait until evening, when there is less chance of attack.

brushed leaves so touch plants as little as possible. Thin carrots, water, and harvest in the evening when these pests are less active.

Harvesting and storage

Dig up early varieties 12 weeks after sowing, maincrops after 16 weeks. Carrots are best eaten fresh; some can also be stored in paper sacks, in boxes of damp sand, or frozen after blanching.

VARIETIES 'Adelaide', 'Amsterdam Forcing', 'Bertan', 'Ideal', 'Maestro', 'Mignon', 'Mini Finger', 'Parmex', 'Resistafly', 'Valor'

Expert tips

- Outfox low-flying carrot fly by planting in pots 60cm (2ft) or more high; otherwise erect fleece barriers around the plants to that height or lift up the pots.

- Maincrop varieties are the best to grow if you want crops for storing.

Beetroot bonanza

Beetroot are refreshingly simple to grow, taste delicious, and make a handsome crop in a pot with their fresh green leaves streaked with red veins and stems. When sown closely for young, sweet roots they almost burst from the pot, just asking to be picked!

There are many more beetroot varieties than the round, ruby-red roots we are all familiar with. There are white ones, striped ones, golden yellow ones, and long, cylindrical types. These are all grown in the same way, although it is best to choose the rounder types when growing in pots. Sow from mid-spring until midsummer; any earlier may cause problems with germination. However, if you cannot wait, sow indoors in modules or under cloches.

Sow a pot every few weeks for a successional harvest and place pots in a sunny spot, although beetroot does tolerate partial shade.

Most beetroot seeds are actually clusters of two or three, but this means they need thinning soon after germination to give the seedlings plenty of space to grow healthily. Do this by cutting surplus seedlings off with scissors, so as not to disturb the ones that are left. When seedlings reach about 2cm (³⁄₄in) high thin them again to their final spacing of 5–10cm (2–4in) – the closer they are spaced, the smaller the roots you will get.

When harvesting pull up individual plants by the leaves and then twist off the foliage rather than cutting it off with a knife – twisting reduces the amount of bleeding of the red beetroot juice. You can use the roots in a variety of ways (see p100). The young leaves go well in salads, and you can steam older leaves as you would spinach.

Beetroot thrives in a pot as long as it is kept watered. Water particularly thoroughly in warm dry weather and when the roots are starting to swell.

Sowing your beetroot seed

What you need

- terra-cotta pot at least 20cm (8in) in diameter and 20cm (8in) deep;
- multipurpose or loam-based potting compost;
- drainage material such as polystyrene chunks, gravel, or broken terra-cotta crocks (see p15);
- beetroot seed such as 'Moneta' or 'Barbabietola di Chioggia' (see p100);
- balanced liquid fertilizer.

1 Line the base with drainage material. Fill the pot with potting compost, firming it with your fingertips. Leave a 5cm (2in) gap between the soil surface and the top of the pot.

2 Water the compost before sowing so the seed won't get washed about later. Sow seed thinly across the top of the compost. Cover with 2cm (³⁄₄in) compost. After sowing, water with a rose so as not to disturb the seed too much.

3 Keep the compost moist. Seedlings should appear within a couple of weeks. Thin them out regularly so by the time the seedlings are about 2cm (³⁄₄in) high they are 5cm (2in) or more apart. Keep your plants well watered and fed.

4 Harvest tender, baby roots when they are the size of golf balls, pulling them sharply by the leaves and taking care not to disturb the remaining plants. This will make room for the other roots to develop further.

Carrots and chives

Sweet, crisp carrots are one of the easiest crops to grow in a pot, as you can make the compost as light and free-draining as these plants need and simply lift the pot onto a table so they grow well out of the way of the dreaded carrot fly. In the open ground, however, conditions are more exacting, and barriers are needed against this pest. Onions (*Allium*) are often used to mask the scent of carrot leaves from the carrot fly, so plant a row of chives (*A. schoenoprasum*) around the edge of the pot as a precaution.

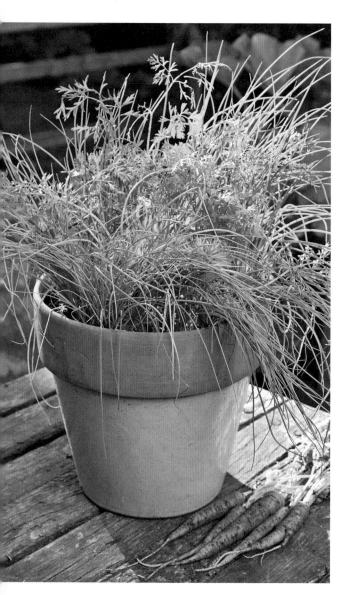

Carrots are best sown directly into their final pot, because, like all root vegetables, they hate to be disturbed, and transplanting can actively damage them. Wait until temperatures start to warm up in spring as the seed won't germinate when the temperature is below 5°C (41°F), and the cooler the temperature the paler and smaller any carrot roots will be. Place the pot in a warm, sheltered spot and make sure it is kept well watered for optimum germination. Sowing a pot such as this every three weeks or so will ensure a steady supply throughout summer rather than one huge glut of roots.

In the constant battle against plant pests and diseases it is always a good idea to grow crops with others if you can, rather than on their own as a monoculture. When alliums, such as onions, garlic, and chives, are grown with carrots, it is thought by many that their strong oniony smell masks the scent of the carrot leaves, and thus the crop may escape the attentions of carrot fly. Also, by growing chives alongside carrots there is the bonus of an extra crop with an oniony punch to add to salads or new potatoes. Chives' edible flowers (see p140) are also adored by bees and will help to attract these helpful pollinators to your garden (see p24).

Carrots and chives are an ideal combination. As the chives are perennial and can stay in the pot, you need to re-sow only the carrots for a constant supply in the growing season.

Planting your carrots & chives

What you need

- chive plant;
- glazed terra-cotta pot 20cm (8in) or more in diameter;
- horticultural grit for drainage;
- multipurpose potting compost;
- carrot seed;
- horticultural sand.

1 Water the chives in their pot. Then remove the plant from its pot and divide it into smaller sections so that you have enough to spread around the new pot. Do this by carefully splitting the plant with your fingers, initially in half and then in half or thirds again.

2 Line the base of the pot with plenty of grit. Then fill it two thirds full with compost. Space the chive sections evenly around the edge of the pot and fill around them with compost. Top up the pot with more compost to about 5cm (2in) below the rim.

3 Water the compost. Then mix the carrot seed with sand and scatter it thinly over the bare compost surface. Sprinkle compost thinly over the seed. Keep the compost moist to aid seed germination. These plants are fairly drought resistant, but keep an eye on watering if conditions are very dry.

4 Give the new carrots room by harvesting a few when very young (see p101). These can be eaten whole in salads. Pick the chive leaves when required, and harvest the remaining carrots once they are larger.

Parsnips

Parsnips require a bit of patience. Germination can be tricky and they are slow to grow, but once they get going they are easy. Either dedicate a pot to them and forget about them or sow between their rows with intercrops of quicker vegetables such as radishes and lettuces. Parsnips can be left in the ground until needed, while frost helpfully turns their starches to sugars. Do not leave them too long though – they'll turn woody and tasteless.

Basic needs

Grow only in large pots, troughs, or tubs, 40cm (16in) or more deep, because parsnips need depth and room for their leafy growth. Mix one part sand with three parts loam-based or multipurpose potting compost.

Growing techniques

1 Sow three seeds at 25cm (10in) intervals but do not sow too early – sowings in late winter are more likely to fail than those in spring.

2 When seedlings are 2cm (¾in) high, thin to one seedling every 15cm (6in).

3 Water well, keeping the potting compost moist to prevent roots from splitting. Feed regularly.

Problem solving

Thanks to canker-resistant cultivars parsnips should be trouble-free.

Harvesting and storage

Parsnips are ready to be dug up when the leaves start to die down in mid- and late winter, although traditionally you harvest after the first frost and continue pulling as you need them through the winter. Peel and cook fresh parsnips; otherwise peel, cut, and blanch before freezing.

VARIETIES 'Albion', 'Arrow', 'Dagger', 'Gladiator', 'Lancer', 'Tender and True'

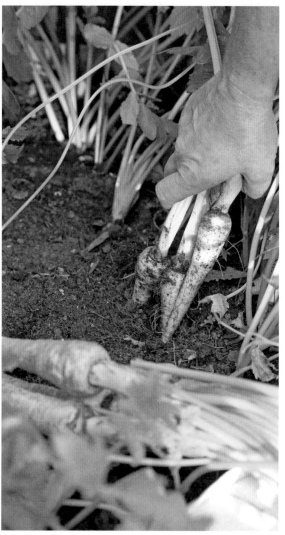

Parsnips are ready to lift from midsummer onward, or may be left in the pot until needed. The longer they remain in the soil the greater the risk of attack by carrot fly.

Expert tips

- Parsnip seed does not retain its viability so use fresh seed every year.
- If eager to sow in late winter warm the soil before sowing with cloches and leave on until the seedlings are well established.

Radishes

Nothing is quicker or easier to grow than radishes – they are a veg plot favourite for good reason! There are crisp, sweet summer varieties ready to harvest in less than a month, and larger, hardier winter types sown toward the end of the summer. Sow summer ones in batches regularly, either in dedicated pots or dotted wherever there's space among other crops, such as parsnips.

Expert tips

- For an early crop warm the compost under cloches before sowing seed in late winter.
- Sow summer varieties thinly – about 2.5cm (1in) apart – and there should then be no need to thin the seedlings.

Basic needs

Grow summer types in pots 10cm (4in) deep, winter ones in pots 20cm (8in) deep, filled with loam-based or multipurpose potting compost.

Growing techniques

1 Sow from early spring until late summer in an open, sunny site. Summer varieties can cope with some shade.

2 Sow summer types thinly; space seed for winter types 20cm (8in) apart.

3 Keep potting compost moist and feed regularly.

Problem solving

Flea beetles can do a lot of damage, peppering the leaves of young seedlings with tiny holes (see p35). It's best to net plants. Slugs and snails can decimate a young crop unless controlled (see p32). Ensure the soil does not dry out to prevent radishes from splitting or bolting.

Harvesting and storage

Summer types are best picked young and eaten straight away. Lift winter varieties as you need them or harvest before the frosts and store. For edible pods let plants flower and pick the pods when crisp and green.

VARIETIES 'Amethyst', 'Cherry Belle', 'French Breakfast', 'Munchen Bier', 'Ping Pong', 'Pink Beauty', 'Rougette', 'Sparkler', 'Zlata'

Either thin radish to give roots room to grow, or thin plants later by harvesting very young, bite-sized roots.

Radishes have a tasty, peppery punch. Munch them freshly harvested from the pot or toss them chopped into salads.

Leeks

Leeks are one of the great winter vegetables and not difficult to grow if you get a few things right. For pots there are special varieties that can be harvested early, when still small, or be left to grow on to develop into ordinary leeks.

Basic needs

Mix 1:3 parts organic matter and potting compost in a large pot, 20cm (8in) or more deep. Avoid grow-bags since they are too shallow for leeks. Baby types can have slightly smaller pots.

Growing leeks in a raised bed or large pot will give you a reasonable harvest whenever you are ready for it.

Growing techniques

1 In spring sow leek seed 10–15cm (4–6in) apart in their final pots. Do not worry about transplanting as you would if growing them in the open ground. Sow a row of baby leeks, 3cm (1¼in) apart, every few weeks during the growing season.

2 Leave room in the top of the pot and gradually fill it up as the leeks grow to blanch the stems.

3 Water leeks in very dry weather.

4 Topdress plants with high-nitrogen fertilizer from mid- to late summer.

Problem solving

Leeks suffer from the usual onion family problem of rust, although it should be only cosmetic. Rust is caused by wet and poor air circulation, so do not overcrowd pots.

Harvesting and storage

Harvest baby leeks when they are the thickness of a pencil, lifting them as required. Dig up maincrop leeks from autumn onward and eat them fresh. There's no need to store them because they can remain in the ground until the following spring, if you have any left!

VARIETIES 'Apollo', 'Atal', 'Imperial Summer', 'Kajak', 'King Richard', 'Longbow', Mammoth Pot', 'Musselburgh', 'Oarsman', Swiss Giant Group, 'Zermatt', 'Toledo', 'Tornado'

Expert tips

- When drawing soil up around the stems to blanch them, try not to let the soil fall in-between the leaves.
- If leek moth is a problem in your area cover young plants with fleece to stop adult moths laying their eggs in the leaves.

Onions & shallots

Onions are cheap to buy, readily available, and take a long time to grow, so concentrate your growing skills on less common, sweet red onions, mellow shallots, and lively spring onions (see p110). Plant a short row or two in a large tub or dot them among other crops. Shallots will give you a bigger crop of smaller bulbs, and spring onions even more – they are also an ideal catch crop.

Basic needs

For a reasonable-sized crop use a large container 20cm (8in) or more deep. For extra nutrients add specialized onion fertilizer to a mix of loam-based potting compost and grit (see p111).

Growing techniques

1 Although onion seed is available, it is easier and quicker to grow all but spring onions from sets (immature bulbs). Plant from early to mid-spring, 10cm (4in) apart, or in early autumn for overwintering. Ensure the pointed end of each onion set is uppermost and the tip just showing. Then water. Sow spring onions at intervals from early spring for a supply through the summer.

2 Onions will bolt if they are not given enough water so mulch to conserve moisture and do not let the soil dry out. Feed plants regularly.

Dry onions in the sun for a couple of weeks to help cure their skins. They will then be ready to store.

Problem solving

Damp, humid, overcrowded conditions can cause fungal diseases such as rust and onion downy mildew, although neither should be devastating. Avoid watering foliage and ensure good light and air around plants.

Harvesting and storage

Spring onions should be ready 8–10 weeks after sowing. Onions and shallots are both ready to harvest when foliage turns yellow and floppy. Leave them for two to three weeks and then carefully lift them with a handfork. Dry them in the sun before storing in bags or trays in a cool, dry place; they will keep several months. Use autumn-planted onions straight away.

VARIETIES onion: 'Marco', 'Red Baron', 'Setton'; shallot: 'Delvad', 'Eschalote Grise', 'Longor', 'Matador', 'Pikant'; spring onion: 'Apache', 'Lilia', 'Ramrod', 'White Lisbon'

Expert tip

- Before planting remove loose skin from each onion set to stop birds pecking at it.

A simple box of spring onions will give you a quick, onion tang to add to all sorts of dishes.

Onion quarters

Onions are one of the most versatile vegetables in the kitchen – you can easily find a use for an onion, shallot, or spring onion every single day. Although you won't be able to grow enough for this in pots, they are a fun and easy crop to cultivate. They make an unusual container display with their upright, glaucous leaf spikes, and in this project look particularly striking against the matt black of a recycled tyre trug.

In a limited space go for a few choice red onions, unusual, expensive-in-the-shops shallots, and a sprinkling of spring onions, sown successively to keep you going through the summer. A late summer sowing of spring onions will be ready to pull again the following spring. Add garlic chives for a gentle tang, which can be snipped right up until autumn. Onion and shallot sets can be planted in autumn or early to mid-spring, depending on variety. Plant the sets in free-draining soil and give them a sunny, sheltered spot. All onions hate sitting in the wet and will quickly rot if they do, so adding grit to the container is a good idea. Stop watering once onions have swollen. They are ready to lift once their leaves begin to yellow, as are shallots; leave them to dry in the sun for a couple of days before using or storing (see p109). Spring onions can be ready in as little as eight weeks after sowing.

Above: Harvest spring onions by pulling them gently by the stems when they are about pencil thickness. They are best eaten fresh – they give a delicious, tangy punch to a salad.

Left: Resist the temptation to overplant your trug, because onions will suffer from fungal diseases if there isn't good air circulation between the plants.

Planting your mixed onion trug

What you need
- recycled tyre trug;
- drill;
- horticultural grit;
- loam-based potting compost;
- specialized onion fertilizer;
- horticultural sand;
- onion and shallot sets, young garlic chive plant, spring onion seed.

1 Make some drainage holes in the base of the recycled tyre trug with a drill. Then line the base of the trug with a generous layer of grit. Fill the trug two thirds full with potting compost and some fertilizer and then add more grit until it is almost at the top of the trug – leave a gap of 5–10cm (2–4in) for watering.

2 Mix the grit evenly into the compost and firm down with your fingers. Then using sand mark out four quarter 'plots'. Push the onion and shallot sets gently into the compost – each in a marked area. Ensure their tips are poking just above the surface and water them in.

3 Plant young garlic chives in spring and sow spring onion seed thinly, giving each crop a dedicated quarter section of its own. Water them in.

4 Always label the crops to aid identification especially as these crops look similar. Every 10–14 days once plants are established topdress with the onion fertilizer and water it in. Water regularly while in growth.

5 Shallots should be ready from mid- to late summer when the leaves begin to flop and yellow (see p109). Leave them for 2–3 weeks before lifting. Dry in the sun for a couple of days then use at once or store them.

Garlic

By growing your own garlic you can try a whole world of new and exciting varieties. There are two basic types: soft neck, which has bendy stems that are easily plaited, produces lots of small cloves, and stores well; and hard neck, which has a hard flower spike running through the middle and bears much bigger cloves. Both types pretty much look after themselves while in growth, and thrive in pots on their own or dotted among other veg.

Basic needs

Grow in a large pot, 40cm (16in) wide, filled with equal parts loam-based potting compost, grit, and garden compost.

Garlic is best planted in late autumn or early winter; in Europe it has always been traditional to plant sets by the shortest day of the year in December.

Once lifted, dry garlic in the sun for a couple of days, before storing indoors, somewhere cool.

Expert tips

- If a plant starts to flower, just snip off its head to focus the plant's energies into producing a large bulb.
- Bulbs may start sprouting and can rot in storage if you delay harvesting.
- Do not bother planting supermarket cloves – you are likely to be disappointed. They are prone to viruses and come from more tender varieties.

Growing techniques

1 Break up the bulbs and plant each clove just below the compost surface. Water well. A spot of cold weather will help bulbs develop.

2 Water garlic in very dry spells but take care not to overdo it. Stop watering when the foliage starts to turn yellow, which means the bulbs are reaching maturity.

Problem solving

Cover plants with fleece to stop birds pecking at the cloves. Long spells of wet weather may cause rust or onion rot. Do not crowd plants to help air circulate freely around them.

Harvesting and storage

Lift bulbs for green garlic in early summer or when leaves turn yellow for more mature bulbs. You can also pick young green leaves earlier for salads, and hard-neck garlic has fancy, looping flowerheads that can be snapped off and eaten. Lift bulbs with a handfork and store in old vegetable crates or weave soft-neck garlic stems into plaits and hang in the cool to dry.

VARIETIES soft-neck: 'Arno', 'Cristo', 'Early Purple Wight', 'Solent Wight', 'Spring Wight'; hard-neck: 'Early Wight', 'Lautrec'

Chard

Chard is one of the most ornamental crops and looks fantastic in pots, particularly if you choose one of the varieties with coloured stems such as 'Bright Lights' or vibrant pink-stemmed 'Rhubarb Chard'. It is difficult to fail with this crop, and it is brilliantly hardy, often lasting right through the winter until it is time to sow a new crop the following spring.

Basic needs

Plants need a pot 20cm (8in) or more deep since they have long taproots, so choose a large container or trough rather than a grow-bag. Use multipurpose or loam-based potting compost, but add a couple of trowelfuls of garden compost or manure to the bottom of the pot to feed the chard roots.

Growing techniques

1 In mid-spring sow seed thinly, 2.5cm (1in) deep. Place the pot in an open site that is preferably sunny. If you have the space sow again in midsummer for crops that can be harvested the following spring.

2 Mulch to conserve water and do not let the potting compost dry out. Feed regularly.

3 Plants may need protection with straw and fleece in cool-temperate areas during winter.

Problem solving

Chard is a toughie and usually trouble-free.

Harvesting and storage

Start to harvest leaves and stems just 10 weeks after sowing. Pick often and when needed to keep new leaves coming, cutting outer leaves first when these are young and tender. Chard keeps for a few days in the refrigerator, but it does not freeze well.

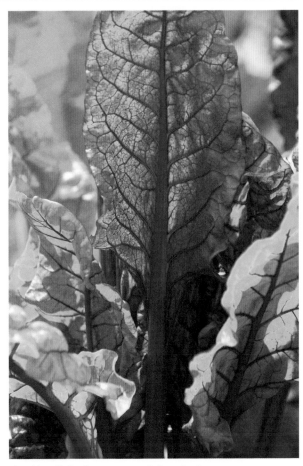

Chard is a distinctive, ornamental plant that keeps on developing edible leaves and stems for use as and when you need them.

Expert tips

- If plants are left to flower the flower stalks can be cooked and eaten in the same way as sprouting broccoli.
- Although chard tolerates some shade you will get a better crop in full sun.

VARIETIES 'Bright Lights', 'Bright Yellow', 'Canary Yellow', 'Charlotte', 'Costa Bianca', 'Fordhook Giant', 'Lucullus', 'Rhubarb Chard'

Spinach

Delicious, nutritious spinach can be picked as small, tender, cut-and-come-again leaves for salads or be allowed to grow bushier for larger leaves for cooking. It grows year-round so is a handy crop to have in a pot when other greens are in short supply. New Zealand spinach, although not a true spinach, tastes almost the same and romps happily through hot summers, when traditional spinach bolts.

Basic needs
Use loam-based potting compost mixed with slow-release fertilizer and grit in a pot 20cm (8in) deep.

Growing techniques
1 Sow thinly every couple of weeks from early spring to early autumn, depending on the variety.

2 Place the pot in a slightly shady spot or grow plants among taller crops so the spinach is kept cool and the potting compost does not dry out too quickly.

3 Thin seedlings only for large-leaved crops.

4 Keep plants watered well and feed regularly.

5 Winter crops may need fleece protection.

Problem solving
They are usually trouble-free apart from attacks on seedlings by slugs and snails (see p32). Plants may bolt if the potting compost is dry.

Expert tips

- Spinach bolts very easily, so stop sowing from early summer, when dry weather can cause problems. Sow winter varieties at the end of the summer.
- To stop leaves tasting bitter make sure the compost has plenty of fertilizer or garden compost added at planting time.

Harvesting and storage
Keep cutting leaves as soon as they are big enough to use, to encourage further growth. Eat straight away; do not bother freezing spinach.

VARIETIES 'Bordeaux', 'Dominant', 'Emilia', 'Lazio', 'Matador', 'Mikado', 'Scenic', 'Toscane'; New Zealand spinach

Sow spinach earlier in the season rather than later to prevent it from bolting, which it does readily in hot, dry weather.

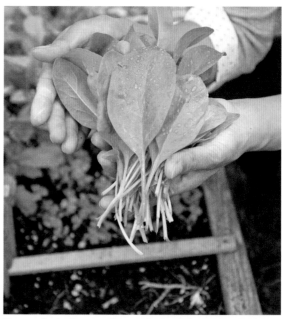

Harvest the fresh, young leaves of spinach for use in mixed salads and sandwiches or lightly steam them in stir-fries.

Rhubarb

Rhubarb is an impressive-looking plant. Although it needs a large container, it is perfectly feasible to grow it in such a restricted environment. You can even get bag kits for rhubarb. It is easy and undemanding; copes well with neglect; and is completely hardy and perennial so it will last a long time. Rhubarb also crops over a long period especially if given a little extra assistance.

Basic needs

Grow each rhubarb crown in a large pot, 60cm (24in) wide and deep, with plenty of drainage holes – old dustbins are ideal.

Growing techniques

1 The best plants are grown from young crowns or divided from mature ones.

2 Plant from mid-autumn to late winter with the growing point at or just below the potting compost surface (see p117). Water plants well.

3 Set the pot in a sunny, frost-free spot.

4 Mulch in spring with well-rotted organic matter to retain moisture, taking care not to bury the crown. Water and feed the plant regularly.

5 Allow the foliage to die back in autumn. Then remove it to expose the growing point to the winter cold.

Problem solving

Look out for limp leaves and weak growth, which is indicative of the fungal disease crown rot. Dig up and bin affected plants.

Harvesting and storage

Pull stems with a twisting motion (see p116), rather than cutting, so you do not leave behind a stump, which will rot. Harvest only half the stems in one go, from spring until midsummer. For an early harvest of pink, tender stems, force plants in mid- to late winter by covering them with a layer of straw and an upturned bucket or dustbin lid.

Rhubarb can be eaten raw, cooked, or frozen when cooked.

VARIETIES 'Hawke's Champagne', 'Raspberry Red', 'Timperley Early', 'Victoria'

Expert tips

- Remove any flowerheads as they appear.
- Do not harvest rhubarb in its first season, and pick only lightly the second year after planting to avoid weakening crowns.
- If forcing rhubarb in spring leave the plant to recover for the rest of the season. You can crop from it again the following year.
- Divide plants after five years, splitting the crown into sections with a spade.

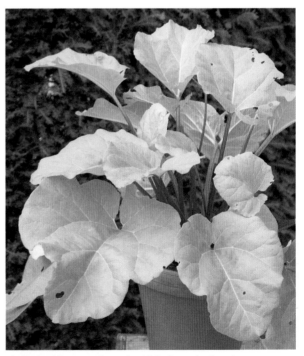

Rhubarb adds an exotic touch with its large, leathery leaves and ruby stems. Remove tired leaves so the plant looks fresh.

Rhubarb for picking

This handsome crop looks fantastic in a pot, adding a certain lushness to a shady spot. Rhubarb needs a big container however, and old dustbins are particularly suitable especially when attractively painted as shown here.

Rhubarb is best grown from young crowns planted between mid-autumn and late winter, although you will need to exert a little patience, because you can't harvest plants in the first year. Otherwise rhubarb doesn't ask for much – just give it food and water and the subsequent harvests will be well worth the wait. It's a deep-rooting plant, which is why dustbins are good, but a single crown will happily grow in a large pot, 60cm (24in) wide and deep. Rhubarb is quite a greedy plant so give it a generous helping of organic matter when planting and keep it well watered in summer. Mulching the plant in spring will also help retain water in the soil (see p115). Rhubarb hates sitting in cold, wet soil so do not give plants any extra water over winter. As a leafy crop rhubarb requires a nitrogen feed rather than a liquid tomato one for fruiting crops, so give it a boost in spring by feeding it with a slow-release fertilizer. Plants also need a frosty winter to produce the best stalks so remove the dead foliage once it has died back to expose the crown to the cold.

Above: Harvest rhubarb by pulling the stalks any time between late spring and the end of summer, taking just a few at a time so as not to weaken the plant.

Right: Rhubarb grows well in any large, deep, well-drained container, such as a dustbin. Be sure to water your plant well during any prolonged periods of dry weather in summer.

Planting your rhubarb

What you need
■ masking tape and drill;
■ dustbin;
■ drainage material (see p15);
■ loam-based potting compost;
■ well-rotted manure or garden compost;
■ rhubarb crown.

1 Space strips of tape evenly around the bottom of the bin to stop your drill from slipping and drill holes through the base. Then line the bottom of the dustbin with drainage material.

2 Mix together well two parts of potting compost to one part manure or garden compost. Fill the bin about three-quarters full with the compost mix.

3 Plant the rhubarb crown, taking care not to set it too deeply – the growing tip should be at or just below the surface of the compost.

4 Water well to help the plant establish and mulch, but take care not to bury the crown of the rhubarb. Feed and water regularly in the growing season. Keep plants dry in winter. Mulch the plant again each spring; do it after watering to help retain moisture.

5 Leave the rhubarb to establish during its first growing season and pick only a few stems in the second year (see p115).

French & runner beans

Beans are one of the prettiest, easiest, and most prolific crops you can grow. They are practically self-sufficient and so rewarding it is almost exhausting keeping up with them, so do not grow too many! Not only are they great for novice growers but they also look fantastic trained up a wigwam in a pot.

Basic needs

Beans are hungry so need equal parts of well-rotted manure and loam-based potting compost. Use as big a pot as you can: at least 20cm (8in) deep and 60cm (2ft) wide for runners; 15cm (6in) deep and 30cm (12in) wide for French beans.

Growing techniques

1 Beans are sensitive to cold so wait to sow outside until late spring or early summer.

2 Place the pot in a warm, sunny, sheltered spot.

3 Support all but dwarf climbers with a wigwam, canes, or trellis and help the young plants by tying stems in loosely to the support until they can climb by themselves (see p121).

4 Keep the potting compost moist at all times, and mulch at the beginning of summer to conserve moisture.

5 Feed plants every week in summer with a liquid tomato fertilizer (see p125).

Birds can peck at runner bean flowers, although they find white ones less attractive than red blooms.

Problem solving

Slugs and snails love the young seedlings so deter them (see p32). Any armies of aphids in early summer can be squished by hand (see p34), and planting marigolds in the pot is said to help deter aphids. Use fresh compost every year to avoid foot and root rot fungal disease.

Harvesting and storage

Pick runners when 15–20cm (6–8in) long and before you see beans swelling inside. French beans are ready when 10cm (4in) long. Both can be blanched and frozen, pickled, or made into chutney. French beans mature into haricot beans, which can be dried and stored. Half-ripe French beans are flageolets; eat these fresh or dried.

VARIETIES borlotti: 'Borlotto Lingua di Fuoco'; dwarf French: 'Golddukat', 'Maja', 'Purple Teepee', 'Safari', 'Speedy', 'The Prince'; climbing French: 'Cobra'; dwarf runner: 'Hestia', 'Pickwick'; climbing runner: 'Celebration', 'Red Flame'

'Hestia' is a dwarf, bushy variety of runner bean that has been bred specifically for growing in pots and containers.

Expert tips

- Lack of moisture causes poor crops, so water regularly and well.
- Mist runner-bean flowers to help them set.
- The more you pick the more beans a plant produces, so keep at it.

Broad beans

Broad beans are an old favourite in the veg garden, a delicious staple that is easy to grow in pots, especially if you choose one of the dwarf varieties that reach half the height of the others. All broad beans are lovely picked young, tender, and sweet and simply must be home-grown to get them at their best.

Basic needs

Broad beans have long taproots so need a pot 20cm (8in) or more deep with good drainage. A large pot, 60cm (2ft) in diameter, is best for a decent crop. Use loam-based potting compost.

Growing techniques

1 Hardy varieties can be sown in autumn, otherwise the main sowing time is early to late spring.

2 Sow seed 5cm (2in) deep, 15–20cm (6–8in) apart. Place the pot in full sun.

3 Support taller plants with canes and string or with peasticks, as they develop.

4 Keep the compost moist at all times. Water especially well as soon as plants start to flower, and feed regularly.

Problem solving

Chocolate spot may appear on the leaves of plants grown too close together, in damp, humid weather. It is mainly a cosmetic problem, as are the distinctive leaf notches made by pea and bean weevils. Mice love digging up the fat seeds, so cover the pots until the seed germinates. Also protect young shoots against slugs (see p32). Remove black bean aphids by hand (see p34).

Harvesting and storage

Broad beans can be eaten at all stages, from small, slender pods to fat beans that need shelling and peeling. Pick regularly and eat fresh, or freeze after blanching.

Expert tips

- Stay one step ahead of aphids by sowing in autumn; in cool-temperate areas protect plants with cloches or fleece over winter.

- Pinch out the top 7.5cm (3in) of plants as soon as pods start to form. It diverts energy into the pods and removes the part of the plant that the black bean aphid loves. (The tops are delicious steamed and buttered, so do not throw them away.)

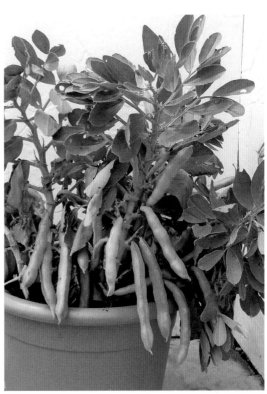

Unlike most broad beans, which are tall and have a tendency to topple over, 'Robin Hood' is a compact variety ideal for growing in containers. Sow in autumn for an early crop.

VARIETIES 'Aquadulce Claudia', 'Crimson Flowered', 'Express', 'Jubilee Hysor', 'Karmazyn', 'Medes', 'Optica', 'Robin Hood', 'The Sutton'

Beans & sunflowers

Runner beans and sunflowers are some of the most rewarding crops to grow together, demanding only a regular supply of water in exchange for beautiful flowers and generous supplies of beans. Together they make a stunning combination and work really well in this large, square granite pot. They also provide a great project for children, who love sowing the large seed and watching these fun crops grow in summer.

Sow this pot when the frosts have passed, in a sunny, sheltered spot. Station sow the seed, planting two at a time in case any fail, and leave at least 10cm (4in) between the sunflower and the bean seeds so that they have plenty of

room to develop. Six plants of each should grow together quite happily in a pot 40cm (16in) wide.

It seems that beans prefer to climb up sunflowers rather than bamboo canes – maybe the hairy plant stems are a better grip for them than those of smooth bamboo. However it is a good idea to support the sunflowers with canes in case they get overwhelmed by the beans. The beans can use the canes as well. Use smaller canes when the plants first start growing and then replace them with taller ones at least the final height of the sunflowers when they reach the top of the cane. If the odd bean ventures on to one of the first, smaller canes gently guide it back to the sunflower stem. Once the taller canes are in place beans can be left to scramble up them. When they reach the top of either the sunflowers or the canes, nip out their tips to stop them growing farther and to keep them cropping well. Regular watering for both of these thirsty crops is vital, particularly when the beans are in flower or the young pods are developing.

Harvest the petals of the sunflowers for salads as the flowers open and leave the seeds to dry on the plant, either for yourself or the birds. Keep picking the beans – the more you do so the more they will continue to produce new beans until the frosts in autumn (see p118).

This dazzling pot is simple to grow, looks stunning, and is extremely productive, providing the grower with a seemingly endless amount of beans at the same time as wowing them with beautiful flowers.

Planting your beans & sunflowers

What you need

- square granite pot, 40cm (16in) or more in diameter;
- drainage material (see p15);
- loam-based potting compost;
- bean and sunflower seed;
- bamboo canes – short and long;
- garden twine.

1 Line the bottom of the pot with drainage material and fill with compost, leaving a 5cm (2in) gap between the rim and the compost. Moisten the compost. Station sow each crop, two seeds at a time for insurance. Then water.

2 Nip out the weaker seedlings at each station after germination. As the plants develop insert canes into the compost as support for the sunflowers. Tie them in with garden twine. Mulch with garden compost (see p118).

3 If by chance a lone bean does start to climb up a short cane, gently guide it back onto the sunflower stem.

4 Once the sunflowers reach the tops of the short canes, replace these with taller ones to ensure the sunflowers have support when the beans start to get heavy. Tie them in well. Mist the bean flowers to aid setting if necessary.

5 Keep these thirsty plants well watered, especially when flowers appear; this may mean watering morning and night in hot weather. Also feed regularly. Nip out the growing tips of the beans when they reach the tops of their supports.

Peas

Home-grown peas are a must for any pot. Their sugars start turning to starch the second they are picked, so it is only by growing your own that you can truly taste fresh peas at their best. The shoots and tips are also delicious in salads – you could even grow pots of peas just for the shoots. And give mangetout and sugar snaps a try; although tall they are quicker-growing than peas.

Basic needs
Grow in a pot 20cm (8in) or more deep, although some container varieties such as 'Half Pint' will crop in a windowbox. They need good drainage, so choose loam-based potting compost and a container with plenty of drainage holes.

Growing techniques
1 Sow wrinkly and round-seeded peas from early spring to early summer, 10cm (4in) apart. Round seed is hardier and can also be sown in autumn. Spread the sowing over a few weeks to avoid any gluts.

For a long, steady supply of sweet, fresh peas, keep picking the plump pods to encourage more to develop.

2 Place the container in an open, sunny spot.

3 Taller pea varieties need something to scramble up – twiggy peasticks, bamboo canes, or netting will help them to cling and climb (see p127).

4 Keep an eye on watering, especially after flowering. Young pods need lots of moisture to swell fully. Feed the plants regularly.

Problem solving
Use netting or start plants off indoors to protect them against pigeons, which tear at leaves and destroy young seedlings, and mice, which can eat the seed before it even has a chance to germinate. Avoid burrowing caterpillars of the pea moth in midsummer by sowing early and late. Do not worry too much about leaf notches left by pea and bean weevils since they should not affect your crop.

Harvesting and storage
Most peas are ready within a couple of months of sowing, when pods are full. Pick mangetout and sugar snaps just as the peas are developing; eat the pods whole. Pod garden peas and eat them raw or cook or freeze straightaway.

VARIETIES 'Balmoral', 'Greensage', 'Half Pint', 'Kelvedon Wonder', 'Misty', 'Purple Podded', 'Serge'; mangetout: 'Oregon Giant', 'Oregon Sugarpod'; sugar snap: 'Cascadia', 'Sugar Ann'

Sweet corn

Sweet corn can be tricky in pots because it is wind-pollinated and needs to be grown in blocks to maximize pollination. However if you have pots that are big enough, it is definitely worthwhile. Mini varieties are perfect for smaller containers – they are harvested before pollination even occurs. The only way to appreciate sweet corn at its absolute best is to grow your own, since its sugars start turning to starch as soon as it is picked.

Basic needs

Grow five or six traditional sweet corn in very large pots and tubs, 20cm (8in) or more deep and 60cm (2ft) or more in diameter. Minis can grow in a slightly smaller pot. Bag kits are also available. Give sweet corn rich soil by mixing three parts potting compost with one part garden compost or organic matter.

Growing techniques

1 Sweet corn needs warmth for germination so sow indoors or under glass. Sow outside once temperatures reach 10°C (50°F) and frosts have definitely passed; or grow from young plants.

2 Plant traditional sweet corn varieties in groups of at least five plants so they can pollinate each other. Place the pots in a sunny, sheltered spot.

3 Ensure the pots are kept well watered and fed. Sweet corn are thirsty plants, especially in pots.

Problem solving

Usually trouble-free.

Harvesting and storage

Pick mini types just before the tassels

Start sweet corn under cover in mid-spring, or sow outside once frosts have passed.

Newer varieties of sweet corn, known as supersweet, have even higher levels of sugar than traditional ones. 'Sweetie Pie' is an early maturing variety that is exceptionally sweet.

appear. Traditional corn is ready when the tassels turn rusty brown and the kernels release a creamy sap – test with your thumbnail (see p124). Twist cobs off the stem just before you eat them; otherwise keep the leaves on the cobs and get them in the refrigerator quickly. Kernels can be cut off, blanched, and frozen. Hang popping corn types up to dry before popping.

VARIETIES 'Minor', 'Mirai', 'Sundance', 'Swallow', 'Sweetie Pie', 'Swift'; mini corn: 'Minipop'; popping corn: 'Strawberry Popcorn'

Expert tips

- Mulch plants to keep in moisture and mound potting compost up over any exposed roots for stability.
- Watering is vital when plants are in flower. Apply liquid feed when cobs start to swell.
- Help pollination by tapping the tassels when they appear.
- Grow only one type of sweet corn in a small space; if mixed, they cross-pollinate and the flavour is reduced.

Beans & sweet corn

Inspired by the American Indian method of companion planting, this large, plastic tub holds elegant canes of sweet corn and dwarf runner beans. In the original system, the beans climb up the sweet corn, but here the bushy habit of the beans provides a living mulch around the base of the sweet corn, keeping the roots cool, the canes stable, and the compost moist.

For drainage material in such a large pot it is a good idea to reuse plastic plant pots rather than lots of crocks or gravel. Such pots are light and will easily fill the bottom of the tub, reducing the amount of compost needed and making the planter easier to move around if you need to. Traditionally sweet corn is grown in blocks rather than rows to help pollination (see p123), so as long as your tub is large enough to give plants room to grow they should crop well grouped together in a pot. Next to each cane plant a dwarf runner bean. The flowers are edible as well as the pods. Be sure to keep on picking the beans as they develop – leaving them on the plant will stop production and shorten your harvest.

Sow seed directly in late spring or early summer, when all danger of frosts has passed. Place the tub in a bright, sunny spot, out of the wind, so that pollinating insects can easily reach the bean flowers. Water these crops well, particularly when they are in flower and when the pods and cobs are developing. Give them a regular weekly liquid tomato feed from this point onward. Mulch around plants in summer (see p118).

Above: Cobs are ready when the tassels turn a rusty brown. Test them for ripeness by sticking a thumbnail in a kernel. If a milky sap is released it is ripe; if it is still clear, leave the cob on the plant for another day or two.

Left: The combination of sweet corn and beans grown together in one pot works really well, with the beans providing nitrogen and protection for the sweet corn. The sweet corn will support the beans and shelter them, and so encourage bees and other pollinating insects to the flowers.

Planting your beans & sweet corn

What you need

■ large, plastic tub 50cm (20in) in diameter;
■ drainage material (see p15) or old plastic plant pots;
■ loam-based potting compost;
■ sweet corn and dwarf runner bean seed.

1 Line the bottom of this large pot with old plastic plant pots or a generous layer of drainage material.

2 Cover the pots with potting compost, filling the tub only to 5cm (2in) below the rim, to leave room for watering. Water the compost.

3 Station sow two sweet corn seeds at each spot to ensure sufficient plants if some fail to germinate. Six or seven plants will fit well in a pot this size, spaced evenly around the sides and across the middle.

4 Sow the runner bean seed in exactly the same way, two seeds per spot, close to the sweet corn so that they will be conveniently placed to grow up each corn stem. Water well. Thin out the weaker seedling of each crop in each spot.

5 Water and feed the plants regularly. Both corn and beans are thirsty plants and may need watering twice a day in hot weather, morning and evening. Eat sweet corn as soon as it is harvested (see p123) and pick beans regularly (see p118).

A summer pot

If you want to try just a few crops for the summer this is a quick and easy combination that will keep you in fresh veg over a number of weeks. The crisp cos lettuce should be ready within eight weeks from sowing, followed by the peas, twining up through the centre, while the ruby red beetroot can be picked as soon as it reaches golf-ball size.

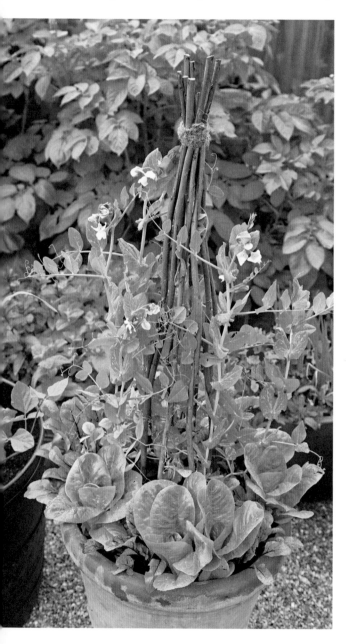

Cos lettuce, with its narrow, upright habit, is a good choice in a limited space. Go for any round beetroot variety, rather than a cylindrical type, which may struggle at the edge of a pot. Any shelling or mangetout variety of pea could be used in this scheme.

Sow your seed directly in the final pot in late spring, placing it in an open, sunny spot. Don't be tempted to sow earlier than this, as pea seed can rot in cold, damp soil. Water the compost before sowing and, to save time thinning lots of seedlings later on, station sow the seed exactly where you want each plant to grow. Give the pot a feed with a balanced liquid fertilizer every two weeks and keep it well watered, especially once the peas are in flower. When the pea seedlings emerge nip out the weakest one of each pair so that there is just one plant per cane.

The lettuces will be ready when each has developed a good, firm heart (see p131). Harvest the first few beetroot when they are baby roots (see p100), and this will give the remaining ones the space to develop into a bigger size if you wish. Keep picking the peas regularly so they are absolutely fresh, harvesting them from the bottom of the plant upward (see p122).

All the crops in this pot can be succession sown in other pots, two or three weeks after these, for a continuous supply of delicious, fresh food.

Planting your summer pot

What you need

- terra-cotta pot 40cm (16in) or more in diameter;
- drainage material (see p15);
- loam-based potting compost;
- bamboo canes;
- garden twine;
- pea, beetroot, and cos lettuce seed.

1 Line the bottom of the pot with drainage material and then top up with compost to about 5cm (2in) below the rim. Firm the compost. Arrange the canes evenly in a circle half way across the pot, leaving space for the beetroot and lettuces to grow around the edge.

2 Bring the tops of the canes together and secure them with twine, winding it around and around before making a knot.

3 Before sowing, water the compost so that it is moist. Sow two pea seeds at the base of each cane, followed by a pinch of lettuce seed and a row of beetroot seed around the edge of the pot. Keep the compost moist while the seed germinates.

4 Thin out the beetroot (see p100) and lettuce seedlings to allow room for the rest to mature. Help the young pea plants up the canes until they can start to cling and twine by themselves. Feed and water plants regularly.

5 Pick the pea pods regularly so they are always young and fresh. Harvest each lettuce when it has a good heart, and the beetroots at whatever size you like them.

Cabbages

There are so many cabbage varieties that you could keep a harvest going through the year, but for container growing it is advisable to stick to the compact types. There are spring, summer, or winter cabbages, and all are grown in the same way – they are just sown and planted at different times of year.

Basic needs

Choose a large container 20cm (8in) or more deep. Grow-bags are not deep enough. Cabbages like rich, firm soil so use equal parts loam-based potting compost, garden soil, and well-rotted organic matter.

Growing techniques

1 Before sowing, firm the compost in the pots down well. Sow thinly.

2 As the plants grow, pull up and firm the potting compost around each bare stem to stop it from toppling over.

3 Keep the plants from drying out and water well as their heads start to form.

4 Apply high-nitrogen fertilizer throughout the growing season.

Problem solving

Keep plants covered with netting to protect them from pigeons, flea beetles (see p35), and cabbage white butterflies. Look out for clusters of eggs on the undersides of leaves and pick off before they hatch into hungry caterpillars, which seem to prefer green cabbages to red types (see p35).

Expert tips

- Multipurpose potting compost is too loosely textured for growing cabbages.
- Cabbages will not heart up unless they are held firmly in the compost.

Harvesting and storage

Gather young leaves for greens as soon as they are big enough. Otherwise wait until the cabbage head has a solid heart, then cut the stem just above the potting compost. Making a cross in the remaining stump will stimulate it to resprout, giving you a second, smaller crop. Winter cabbage can be left to stand in the pot until you are ready to eat it, but cut other types before the first frosts of autumn and store in net bags. Cabbage does not freeze.

VARIETIES green: 'Pixie', 'Minicole', 'Shelta'; red: 'Redcap', 'Rodeo'

Cabbages need firm compost around their bases to keep them upright and help them form good, strong hearts. Keep drawing up the compost and firming around plants.

Small, compact types are great for containers – harvest young leaves or allow cabbages to form dense hearts.

Kale

This great, hardy, winter vegetable is one of the easiest leafy vegetables to grow – it can cope with cold weather better than other brassicas and is finally gaining the popularity it deserves. Attractive, curly, dwarf kale works really well in pots and will provide plenty of delicious pickings throughout winter and spring.

Basic needs
Likes well-drained, nutrient-rich potting compost in a pot 20cm (8in) or more deep.

Growing techniques
1 Sow seed thinly from mid-spring to midsummer in rows, or dot plants among other crops.

2 Mulch to conserve water and do not allow plants to dry out.

3 Feed young plants once to give them a boost.

4 When established, pick leaves regularly to keep young growth coming and nip out flower shoots.

Problem solving
Net plants if birds are a problem – it is said birds prefer the green types of kale to the red ones.

Harvesting and storage
Some kale plants can be harvested as cut-and-come-again salad crops. Start picking these once the plants are 5cm (2in) tall; more young leaves will grow. Pick other types when leaves are young and tender – initially harvest the top ones, from early autumn. Once the crown has been harvested, pick new sideshoots from mid-winter to late spring, until plants go to seed. Eat leaves fresh or store in a refrigerator for a few days.

VARIETIES black: 'Nero di Toscana'; green: 'Afro', 'Bornick', 'Fribor', 'Red Russian', 'Reflex', 'Starbor', 'Winterbor'; red: 'Redbor'

Kale is a must-have crop that is easy, full of flavour, and nutritious. Plant it alone or among other crops.

Kale keeps on producing leaves if picked regularly. A couple of pots should give a constant supply of fresh, tender leaves.

Lettuces & salads

Lettuces are quick, easy to grow, ridiculously productive, and bring a fantastic range of colour and texture to as small or large a container as you wish to use. Although there are hearting types, such as cos, and loose-leaved ones, all can be picked as cut-and-come-again plants that will continue cropping for months and make the most enticing mixed salads. And if you choose the right varieties you can grow salads year-round. Devote whole pots to salads or dot plants among other crops while waiting for them to come up.

Basic needs

Grow in any container 10cm (4in) or more deep, including a windowbox, pot, trough, or grow-bag. Fill with three parts multipurpose potting compost mixed with one part garden compost.

Growing techniques

1 Sow spring and summer salads from early spring, in short rows every couple of weeks for a steady supply and to reduce gluts. They are good grown as cut-and-come-again plants because this minimizes their chances of bolting in hot, dry weather. For winter and early spring leaves sow seed in late summer and early autumn, and cover plants with cloches.

2 Place the containers of lettuces and other salad crops in full sun or a bright, well-lit site.

3 Water well in dry weather in the mornings, to prevent leaf scorch as well as attacks by slugs, which are more likely if plants are watered in the evening. Too little water can make hearting lettuces bolt. Winter lettuces can be pretty much left to cope on their own provided that they are moist. All lettuces need regular feeding.

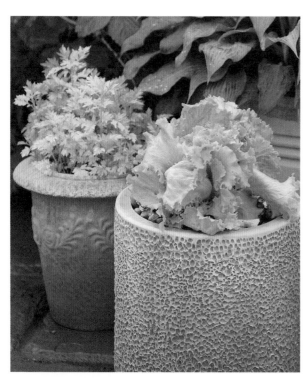

Hearting lettuces are brilliant dotted anywhere you have room – among other crops or occupying the odd spare pot.

Grow rows of colourful and differently shaped, cut-and-come-again leaves for a regular supply of mixed salad.

Containers filled with mizuna, lettuce, and mustard provide tasty mixtures and are especially attractive when flowers such as forget-me-not (*Myosotis*) are added.

Problem solving

Slugs and snails adore young seedlings, so protect pots and plants particularly well at this vulnerable stage of development (see p32). Damp, cold summers may result in grey mould. Pick off infected growth when you spot it and do not plant too densely. Lettuces are prone to bolt in hot, dry weather.

Harvesting and storage

Hearting lettuces are ready as soon as a firm heart has formed. Cut with a sharp knife in the morning when they are fresh. Only harvest cut-and-come-again leaves when you need them; they will not stay fresh for long. Cut leaves from the base with scissors, taking a few from each plant. If you need to store them dampen with water and keep in a plastic bag in the refrigerator.

Expert tips

- Water potting compost before sowing rather than after, to ensure seed is in contact with moist soil (see p132).

- Lettuces like sun but need cool to germinate so if sowing in the hottest months place pots in the shade, sow in the morning, and water with cool water.

- Sow seed closely for cut-and-come-again crops; set farther apart if leaving to heart.

- Water regularly so the compost is moist. As soon as lettuce is stressed it bolts.

VARIETIES chicory: 'Indigo'; corn salad; hearting lettuce: 'Claremont', 'Little Gem', 'Pinokkio', 'Ravel', 'Sunny', 'Winter Density'; loose-leaf lettuce: 'Cocarde', 'Green Oak Leaf', 'Red Salad Bowl'

Summer-long salads

Growing your own mixed salad is simple and can be done at a fraction of the cost of the pre-packed bags available at the supermarket. Sow a mixture of hearting varieties and cut-and-come-again leaves into wooden boxes, such as recycled crates, and you will have a handy supply of fresh leaves that can sit anywhere, even on a windowsill.

Lettuces and other salad leaves are brilliantly undemanding crops that can be sown any time between spring and late summer. With protection from fleece or cloches, crops can even be sown in autumn for picking throughout winter. Before you fill any wooden container with potting compost always line it with plastic – something like an old compost bag is perfect – to stop the wood from rotting and to prevent any preservatives in the wood leaching into the compost. After germination you need to thin hearting types to give them room to develop, but don't waste the thinnings – these can be eaten too. Cut-and-come-again leaves are harvested sufficiently young that they don't need further thinning, provided that they are sown thinly in the first place. Place your crates in sun or dappled shade (see p131) and keep the compost moist, especially in a hot summer, as some salad crops run to seed in the blink of an eye.

Opposite: Sow a box of salad every couple of weeks for a continuous supply of fresh leaves throughout the summer.

Sowing your salad box

What you need
- recycled wooden crate or box; ■ plastic liner; ■ scissors; ■ drainage material (see p15); ■ multipurpose potting compost; ■ garden compost; ■ dibber; ■ salad seed – ready mix combinations and single varieties (see p131).

1 Line the wooden box with the plastic and cut drainage holes in the liner with scissors. Cover the base with drainage material. While filling the box with a mix of the two composts (see p130), hold the liner tightly to each edge of the box. Water the compost.

2 Make two or three shallow drills in the compost using either a wooden dibber or your finger. Take a pinch of seed and sprinkle it thinly along each drill and then draw the compost over the seed with your finger and thumb.

3 When the seedlings of hearting types are 2cm (³/₄in) high thin them so that you have four or five plants per row. Water and feed lettuces regularly. Protect them from slugs and snails (see p32).

4 Harvest cut-and-come again leaves regularly once they are about 5cm (2in) high (see p131), or let them grow to about 15cm (6in), giving them a light thin so plants have more space. You can then cut their entire heads off.

5 Traditional hearting lettuces are picked whole in one go by pulling up the whole plant or by cutting plants with a sharp knife just above the surface of the compost.

Oriental leaves

Oriental leaves is a catch-all term for an increasingly popular group of leafy veg and salads such as pak choi, Chinese cabbage, and mizuna. All are full of punch and texture and are very useful in the kitchen. They can be grown as large heads or as cut-and-come-again baby leaves. Most Oriental leaf vegetables will provide you with fresh leaves from midsummer to early winter.

Basic needs

Most types need a pot 15cm (6in) or more deep filled with good-quality, moisture-retentive soil. Devote a whole pot to Oriental leaves or dot plants among other crops.

Growing techniques

1 Sow thinly from mid-spring to midsummer in a sheltered, sunny place (see p137).

2 Keep the plants well watered and fed to prevent bolting and improve flavour. Chinese cabbage has shallow roots so water little and often.

Problem solving

Slugs love the young leaves and can reduce the

Expert tip

■ Cover plants with fleece or cloches in autumn to extend your harvesting period.

heart of a Chinese cabbage to mush so always control them (see p32). Protect Chinese cabbage against cabbage white caterpillars and flea beetles with netting (see p35).

Harvesting and storage

Most are quick growers: pick cut-and-come-again baby leaves just a couple of weeks after germination; whole plants should be ready for harvesting after about 10 weeks. Leaves will not keep well so gather only what you need. Stumps of most whole plants will resprout giving you more young leaves for a second or third harvest. Use the leaves in salads, stir-fries, or broths.

VARIETIES Chinese cabbage: 'Kasumi', 'One Kilo', 'Yuki'; giant red mustard; mibuna; mizuna; pak choi: 'Canton Dwarf', 'Purple', 'Summer Breeze', 'Tah Tsai', Tatsoi'

Mizuna will grow and grow, no matter how much you cut it, even continuing through winter in warm-temperate areas.

The leaves of mibuna can get tough when plants bolt in hot weather. Their flavour is slightly hotter than that of mizuna.

Rocket

Punchy, peppery rocket is a simple salad crop that can also be cooked and has edible flowers. There are salad and wild types; all are easy to grow, which is great news considering how much rocket costs to buy in the shops.

Basic needs
Grow in a pot, trough, windowbox, or grow-bag, 10cm (4in) deep, filled with loam-based potting compost.

Growing techniques
1 Sow thinly in a slightly shaded spot, from mid-spring to early autumn (see p155).

2 Thin seedlings to 10cm (4in) apart.

3 As plants bolt easily, sow rocket every couple of weeks. Protect autumn sowings over winter in cool-temperate climates with cloches or fleece.

4 Keep rocket watered to stop plants running to seed, but do not overdo it – too much water dilutes the taste. Feed plants regularly.

5 Nip out the flower buds – they are edible too.

Problem solving
Flea beetles can get very bad, defoliating the plants (see p35). Use a fine-mesh net.

Rocket flowers are pretty *en masse*. If you leave your last crop to self-seed you will have new plants next year.

Harvesting and storage
Rocket is ready to crop in as little as four weeks from sowing. Harvest it as a cut-and-come-again crop or as whole plants. Pick often to keep growth tender. Eat leaves fresh or make into rocket pesto.

VARIETIES 'Apollo', 'Buzz', 'Runway', 'Skyrocket', 'Sweet Oakleaf', 'Wild Grazia'

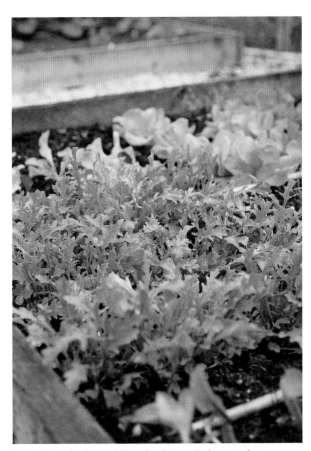

Both wild and salad varieties of rocket can be harvested as cut-and-come-again leaves or entire plants can be plucked.

Expert tip
- Allowing some plants to set seed is a good way to extend and increase your crop.

Some like it hot

Asian food is renowned for its spicy kick, which you can recreate if you fill this simple terra-cotta pot full of the flavours of the Orient. Fresh chillies will add a fiery punch to curries or soups, while the peppery leaves of mizuna and mibuna give a lively note to salads. Mature leaves of pak choi are excellent in Asian broths and its baby leaves for use in stir-fries. The fresh leaves of Asian greens look lovely against terra cotta, and they work just as well in a plastic windowbox near the kitchen to keep everything handy.

Chilli peppers take a long time to grow and ripen over the summer. The hotter the temperatures the quicker they will mature (see p83), but if the weather is poor it can take until autumn before peppers are ripe. To give yourself a head-start

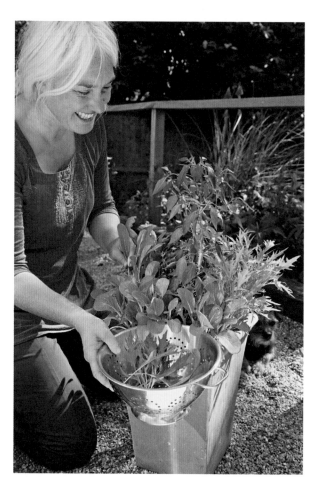

you might prefer to buy chillies as young plants from the garden centre or by mail order and plant them out directly into the final pot when frosts have passed. Set them in your warmest, sunniest spot. Pinch out the growing tips after planting to encourage bushy growth and give your plant liquid tomato fertilizer every week after the flowers appear. To enhance your crop, you can pollinate the flowers yourself (see p86). Depending on variety, plants may need staking as they grow to avoid them becoming top-heavy with fruit and the branches snapping.

Mizuna and mibuna are two of the easiest and most rewarding crops you can grow (see p134). As long as they are picked regularly and any flowering growth is nipped out before they bolt they will go on and on producing fresh, tangy leaves. Pak choi however is particularly prone to bolting, especially in times of stress, usually drought, so ensure the pot is kept well watered. If you are worried about premature bolting, try specially selected seed that has been chosen for strong growth (which includes bolt resistance), good germination rates, and pest and disease resistance. It is more expensive than ordinary seed but is much more likely to succeed. Each seed should germinate so there is no need to oversow to ensure you have enough plants.

Harvest mibuna and mizuna leaves whenever you need them – they start to deteriorate quickly after picking. Both plants should grow strongly, and in milder areas will carry on right through the winter.

Planting your Asian greens

What you need
- terra-cotta pot 30cm (16in) in diameter;
- drainage material (see p15);
- multipurpose potting compost;
- chilli pepper plant;
- mibuna, mizuna, and pak choi seed.

1 Line the bottom of the pot with drainage material and fill it with compost until it is three-quarters full. Plant the chilli pepper in the centre of the pot at the same level it was in its previous pot and fill in with more compost. Water well.

2 Make a shallow drill along each edge of the pot with your finger and sow two sides with mibuna seed and one side with mizuna seed, covering the seed as you go.

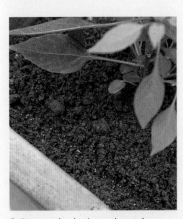

3 Sow pak choi seed on the fourth side. Cover it with potting compost so that it is at the depth recommended on the seed packet.

4 Water the seed in well to help establishment and germination. Then keep the compost moist – never let it dry out. Feed the plants regularly. Protect the young plants against slugs and snails (see p32).

5 Thin the seedlings to allow individual plants to grow strongly. Pak choi needs more room than mizuna and mibuna, which can be harvested as cut-and-come-again leaves (see p134). Eat the tasty thinnings in salads. Harvest the first chillies when they are green (see p87).

Herbs

Both the flowers and slender, tubular leaves of chives are edible, adding a tangy, onion punch to any meal.

Chives

Chives (*Allium schoenoprasum*), with their fresh, onion bite, are indispensable in the kitchen, easy to grow, and very happy in pots. Their neat, edible, pompom flowers are loved by bees and other pollinators (see p24).

Basic needs
Given a minimum depth of 10cm (4in), chives will thrive in containers, hanging baskets, and windowboxes. Use loam-based potting compost as chives prefer rich, moist to well-drained soil.

Growing techniques
■ Sow seed in early spring, placing the pot on a sunny windowsill at 20°C (68°F); transplant

outside once there is little risk of frosts. Alternatively sow directly outside from late spring to early summer.

Bees and other pollinating insects buzz merrily around chives' flowers in summer.

■ Chives cope with sun and partial shade.

■ Mulch in spring and nip out flowerheads before they fade to encourage leaf growth.

■ Every 2–3 years divide clumps in spring (see p105) or replace plants.

Problem solving
Overcrowding can make plants susceptible to rust, which causes bright yellow spots on the leaves. Cut infected plants back straight away.

Harvesting and storage
Chives can be harvested once they are 15cm (6in) high by cutting leaves 3cm (1¼in) from the base. Continue harvesting until the first frosts.

VARIETIES 'Corsican White', 'Pink Perfection'; *A. tuberosum*

Dill

Feathery foliage and sprays of yellow flowers make dill (*Anethum graveolens*) a very pretty centrepiece in a mixed herb pot. Its fresh, mild leaves and sharper seeds are outstanding in soups and salads. Dill flowers attract beneficial insects. Do not grow near fennel as these plants cross-pollinate and their offspring will have diluted flavours.

Basic needs
Fill any pot of 30cm (12in) diameter or more with multipurpose potting compost mixed with grit.

Growing techniques
■ Sow seed directly into pots outside after the frosts, or plant out young plants.

■ Grow in a sheltered spot with a little shade.

■ Keep picking for fresh growth and compact, bushy plants. Never cut dill right back.

■ Dill is short-lived and bolts if even slightly dry, so grow successively for a constant supply.

■ Stake whole plants if necessary, using peasticks and twine.

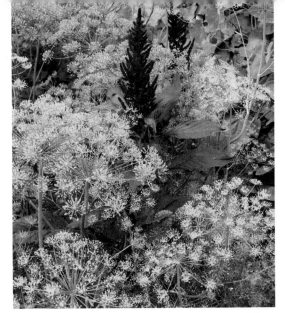

Allow dill to run to flower at the end of the season and then pick the seedheads for drying just as they ripen.

Problem solving

Slugs and snails adore dill so take protective measures around your container and plants to keep these pests away (see p34).

Harvesting and storage

Leaves can be picked about two months after sowing. Eat them fresh, store in the refrigerator for a couple of weeks, or freeze leaves, chopped and mixed with water, in ice-cube trays. Once seed starts to ripen pop stems in a paper bag to dry. They will all ripen at the same time, so be quick off the mark. Store in an airtight container.

VARIETIES 'Diana', 'Herkules', 'Tetra'

Horseradish

Horseradish (*Armoracia rusticana*) is much better when grown in a pot, because it is invasive and tenacious in open soil. It is an easy, unfussy, fully hardy perennial that will provide you with a regular supply of fresh, peppery roots that you are very unlikely to find in the shops. It will last for several years.

Harvest the roots of horseradish by lifting plants in autumn. Use what you need and store the rest in damp sand before planting them again in spring.

Basic needs

Needs a large, deep tub, pot, or old dustbin. Fill with loam-based potting compost that has been mixed with grit, for drainage.

Growing techniques

■ Sow seed; or root cuttings (thongs), 15cm (6in) long, in dibbled holes in potting compost. The cutting will grow whichever way up you plant it.

■ Horseradish likes a sunny site, but tolerates a little shade.

■ Water in dry periods and feed with seaweed fertilizer during summer.

Problem solving

Cover with netting to stop cabbage white caterpillars munching on the leaves (see p35).

Harvesting and storage

Young leaves can be picked for use fresh or dried, and roots can be divided or dug up when needed. Alternatively lift the whole plant for harvest in autumn and store the roots in boxes of sand for use later or for planting again as thongs in spring to create new plants. Roots can be grated or sliced when fresh or be stored in vinegar. They also keep in the refrigerator for up to a week. Horseradish loses its flavour completely if cooked.

VARIETIES 'Variegata'

Coriander

This distinctive, pungent annual has gorgeous leaves and wonderful seeds – even the flowers and roots are edible. Coriander (*Coriandrum sativum*) is easily grown from seed and is a bargain in terms of cropping potential.

Basic needs
Use a well-drained pot, 10cm (4in) deep, filled with multipurpose potting compost.

Growing techniques
■ Sow seed from spring onward. Wait until there is little risk of frosts if you wish to sow outside (see p144).

■ Choose a warm but shaded spot (see p144) if growing for leaves; seeds ripen best in full sun.

■ Sow successional pots, every 3–4 weeks.

■ Keep plants well watered because coriander bolts at the slightest upset. Liquid feed every two weeks through the growing season.

Problem solving
Tends to be trouble-free.

Coriander is quick to run to seed so grow pots of it successionally or sow it at intervals dotted among other crops for a continuous supply.

Harvesting and storage
Cropping can begin as soon as leaves are large enough – generally 7–9 weeks after sowing. Use leaves fresh or freeze them in ice-cube trays. In autumn cut the seedheads when they are almost ripe and put in paper bags to dry; then store the seed in airtight containers.

VARIETIES 'Calypso', 'Confetti', 'Leisure', 'Lemon', 'Morocco'

Lemongrass

This increasingly popular herb is often used in Asian cuisine for its sweet, lemony scent. The striking canes of lemongrass (*Cymbopogon citratus*) look graceful in pots.

Basic needs
Needs a large pot at least 40cm (16in) wide. Mix grit into garden or loam-based potting compost.

Growing techniques
■ Grow lemongrass outside only where night temperatures do not fall below 13°C (55°F); otherwise cultivate them indoors.

■ Grow from young plants or by rooting a stem in a glass of water then planting it up. Sow seed at 20°C (68°F); it takes 2–3 weeks to germinate.

■ Do not let plants dry out in summer, and give a weekly liquid feed through the growing season.

■ Plants will go dormant once temperatures and light levels start to drop, so reduce watering and cut leaves back to 10cm (4in) above the stems.

■ Protect lemongrass from frost over winter.

■ Divide plants by gently teasing apart with your fingers. Pot up straight away into a container that fits snugly round the roots – lemongrass loves to be pot-bound.

Problem solving
Keep plants practically dry and frost-free in winter since they are prone to mildew (see p34) and rot.

Lemongrass is ideal in a container in cool-temperate climates, so it can be moved indoors for protection over winter.

All parts of this aniseed-flavoured plant are edible, including the seeds, which can be eaten both fresh and dried.

Harvesting and storage

Both leaves and stems can be harvested throughout the growing season to be used fresh or dried. Cut the stems at soil level and use the bottom 10cm (4in) of each stem.

VARIETIES Only the species is grown.

Fennel

Closely related to the bulbous Florence fennel, this feathery fennel (*Foeniculum vulgare*) is grown for its perky, aniseed leaves, seeds, and even its flowers. When dotted through a large, mixed container, this airy plant makes a stunning feature. Coloured foliage varieties are particularly attractive.

Basic needs

Plant in any pot, tub, or windowbox, 30cm (12in) deep, that has plenty of drainage holes. Give fennel well-drained, moisture-retentive potting compost, with some grit mixed in. Never grow fennel too near dill or coriander – they cross-pollinate, and their offspring have less flavour.

Growing techniques

■ Purchase young plants, or sow seed directly outside, from mid-spring to early summer.

■ Give fennel a sunny spot.

■ Water regularly and mulch around plants with garden compost. This will stop the fennel plants going to seed too quickly.

■ For a supply of fresh, young leaves remove the flowerheads at once and shorten stems to 30cm (12in) above ground level in midsummer.

■ Remove old stems after plants have died back.

Problem solving

Keep an eye out for slugs, which love the young shoots. Hide beer traps in pots (see p32).

Harvesting and storage

Everything is edible. Pick the leaves, young stems, and unripe seeds to use fresh when you need them. Ripe seeds can be dried and stored for use later. Leaves can be frozen as well as infused in oil or vinegar as a flavouring.

VARIETIES 'Purpureum', 'Rubrum'

Coriander in a colander

Coriander is a fast, easy crop that lasts only a few weeks, so sow a fresh pot every month for a constant supply throughout summer. Fortunately the entire plant is edible, and the delicious, fragrant seeds can be added to curries and stews. A recycled colander is an ideal container for crops that love free-draining soil.

Coriander is best sown directly where it is to be grown, rather than in a smaller pot and potted on, since it hates having its roots disturbed. Wait until all frosts have passed and then sow seed into free-draining potting compost. A multipurpose one is fine for a short-term crop such as this. Place the container where it will be in shade for some of the day – plants will quickly bolt if in full sunlight all day – but they do need warmth. Coriander is best sown little and often, because it bolts readily when the soil dries out (see p142), and this way you will not waste your crop. Keep sowing fresh supplies until late summer. Plants should be ready to crop 7–9 weeks after sowing. Pick regularly to encourage fresh, young leaves and healthy, compact plants; such harvesting methods will also stop coriander from flowering. Coriander hates damp soil so water it in the morning rather than at night.

Opposite: Coriander is a lush, bright crop that imparts its distinctive fragrance and lemony flavour to Asian and Indian cooking and is also delicious in salads and sandwiches.

Planting your coriander

What you need
- hanging basket liner;
- aluminium colander or any pot 10cm (4in) or more deep with good drainage;
- scissors; ■ square of plastic from an old compost bag;
- multipurpose potting compost; ■ coriander seed.

1 Place the liner in the colander. You may need to trim around the edge and overlap the liner inside to get it to fit. Lay a square of plastic in the centre to help retain some moisture.

2 Fill the colander with compost and firm it down gently with your fingers until the compost is about 5cm (2in) below the rim. Leaving this gap at the top will make watering easier.

3 Space the coriander seed evenly over the compost. Then gently push them in, just into the compost surface.

4 Sprinkle compost over the seed, sieving it through your fingers to give a light dusting. Water well and place the colander in a warm spot in the garden with partial shade during some of the day. Keep the compost moist at all times.

5 Feed plants regularly (see p142). Pick coriander leaves often. When plants start to go to seed, you can either dispose of the plant or allow the seed to develop until it's almost ripe, then cut off the entire seedhead and hang it somewhere warm to dry.

Herbal windowbox

Fresh herbs are bursting with flavour and packed full of vitamins and essential oils. They are expensive to buy but very easy to grow yourself, so a simple windowbox full of herbs is a must-have. Add the smiling faces of some edible pansy flowers to your display and you have an extra-colourful dimension you just won't find in the shops. Keep the windowbox close to the kitchen so you can snip off fresh leaves whenever you need them.

All of these plants can be grown from seed. Parsley is notoriously erratic and slow to germinate (see p153). Both fennel (see p143) and parsley hate being moved, so for best results buy small plants from the garden centre once the weather has warmed up in late spring. Parsley is a biennial, so you'll need to buy a fresh supply for your pots every year, but if grown in a sheltered spot it should give you fresh leaves almost year-round. Fennel is an airy, aromatic perennial,

grown for its warm, aniseed-flavoured leaves, seeds, and flowers. Fennel may need staking to keep it looking good and should be repotted every year. Pansies are undemanding, edible flowers that grow well in loose, rich soil and have a sweet, grassy tang.

Opposite: Place the windowbox in a warm, sheltered spot with some light shade to stop your parsley bolting. Warmth will help to generate the essential oils that give herbs their distinctive flavour and aroma.

Planting your herbal windowbox

What you need
■ windowbox, at least 60 x 20cm (24 x 8in), that fits comfortably and is level on your windowsill;
■ drainage materials such as pieces of broken terra-cotta pots, clay pebbles, or gravel (see p15);
■ loam-based potting compost and grit, mixed 2:1;
■ 2 x parsley (*Petroselinum crispum*), 2 x fennel (*Foeniculum vulgare*), 2 x pansies (*Viola x wittrockiana*).

1 Drainage is important for herbs so punch holes in the base of your windowbox if necessary. Then line the bottom of the box with a generous layer of drainage material.

2 Half fill the box with potting compost. Then, while they are still in their pots, arrange the plants in your windowbox until you are happy with the way they look. Alternating the herbs and then dotting the pansies in-between works well.

3 Remove each plant in turn from its pot, starting with the tall fennel. Gently tease out its roots to help them spread out and establish quickly when replanted. Then plant the parsley and finally insert the pansies among the herbs.

4 Top up the box with compost. Water well and mulch, then place the box on the windowsill. During the growing season water the plants and feed them every week with a balanced liquid fertilizer. Pick the leaves and flowers little and often, to promote growth.

Hyssop is the perfect choice for a pot on a patio, where its lovely scent can be enjoyed on warm, sunny days.

Hyssop

It can be difficult to buy hyssop (*Hyssopus officinalis*), so grow your own supply of this classic Mediterranean herb. The whole plant is deliciously aromatic, especially on hot summer evenings. Its vivid blue, white, or pink flowers attract butterflies and bees.

Basic needs

Grow in any pot, of 30cm (12in) diameter or more, with plenty of drainage holes. Prefers light, well-drained potting compost mixed with grit.

Growing techniques

■ Sow directly into sun-warmed soil in late spring or buy young plants.

■ Loves a sunny spot against a south-facing wall.

■ Trim the plants back in spring. Feed regularly with comfrey fertilizer once flowers appear, and deadhead promptly to keep hyssop flowering.

■ Protect plants in winter with fleece, straw, or bracken if temperatures fall below -5°C (23°F).

■ Replace plants every four years.

Problem solving

Tends to be trouble-free.

Harvesting and storage

Pick leaves from the top to encourage bushy growth. Use fresh, dried, or preserve in olive oil. Harvest flowers just as they open; they are lovely in salads or drinks.

VARIETIES f. *albus*, subsp. *aristatus*, 'Roseus'

Bay

The dark green, evergreen leaves of bay (*Laurus nobilis*) are an essential ingredient in a bouquet garni, so keep this plant by the kitchen door for easy pickings.

Basic needs

Grow in any container, 30cm (12in) or more deep, filled with rich, gritty, loam-based potting compost for good drainage and stability.

Growing techniques

■ Buy young plants, as seed germination is erratic and cuttings can be difficult to propagate.

■ Plant between mid-spring and early autumn in a bright, sheltered spot. Water plants well.

■ Give a liquid feed every couple of weeks from mid-spring to late summer. Water sparingly, particularly in winter – raising the pot on bricks helps water drain away easily.

■ If temperatures drop below 5°C (41°F) protect with fleece. Plants get hardier as they get older.

■ Repot every two years.

Problem solving

Yellow leaves could be caused by a nutrient deficiency, waterlogged potting compost,

The fresh leaves of bay are one of the herbs in a bouquet garni, for use in stews, sauces, and soups. The other popular ingredients are oregano, basil, and thyme.

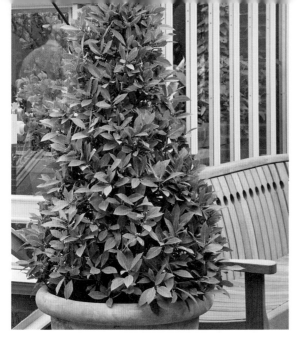

Pot-grown bays can be kept in check by trimming with secateurs into cones, pyramids, or standards.

or harsh weather. Scale insects cause an ugly, sooty mould; wipe off by hand or wash with insecticidal soap. Bay suckers distort and thicken leaves; cut back affected branches.

Harvesting and storage

Pick the foliage year-round. Fresh leaves have a stronger flavour than dried. Bay leaves dry well and can also be preserved in vinegar.

VARIETIES 'Aurea', f. *angustifolia*

Mint

Another tenacious garden invader, mint (*Mentha*) is much better grown in containers. This essential kitchen herb has different scents, flavours, and leaf shapes, most of which are unavailable in the shops.

Basic needs

Needs a minimum container depth of 15cm (6in) and rich, gritty potting compost (see p14).

Growing techniques

■ Grow from young plants, or root cuttings from established ones by digging up a piece of root in the growing season, and cutting by a green node. Place in a pot of seed compost. Water well.

■ Give plants semishade, or a sunnier spot if growing a coloured-leaf type.

■ Ensure different mints are not grown close by, or they hybridize and their offspring lose flavour.

■ Liquid feed regularly during the growing season and do not let potting compost dry out.

■ Deadhead regularly. Tidy up plants in summer.

■ Divide plants every three years.

Problem solving

If you see the brown leaf spots of mint rust, destroy the plant; do not replant in the same pot.

Harvesting and storage

Use fresh leaves throughout the growing season or freeze, rather than dry them.

VARIETIES *M.* x gracilis 'Variegata', *M.* x *smithiana*, *M. spicata*, *M. s.* var. *crispa* 'Moroccan', *M. s.* 'Tashkent', *M. suaveolens*, *M. s.* 'Variegata', *M.* x *villosa* var. *alopecuroides*

Mentha suaveolens 'Variegata' (top left) is slow-growing and perfect for use in a pot. The leaves of *M.* x *gracilis* 'Variegata' (above left) have a warm, gentle flavour, while *M. spicata* (above right) is the best mint for sauces and jellies.

Mint medley

Thanks to their thuggish tendencies mints are often thought of as the baddies of the herb world, but a neat trick is to grow them in pots to stop them rampaging over other plants. This applies even when growing with other mints. To enjoy a range of their pungent leaves grow different mints (see p149) in separate pots inside a single, large pot or other planter. Mint is a shallow-rooting plant, so there is no point in planting it in a very deep pot.

Plant this seasonal project in spring, using light, gritty potting compost, both in the pots and within the larger planter. Before plunging the individual pots into the final planter, pot each mint plant on into a larger container to allow it a little room to spread. The mint roots will soon grow through the bottom of their pot into the compost below. Place the planter in partial shade – you don't want this leafy crop to dry out too quickly. Feed plants regularly (see p149).

By growing mints closely together there is a risk they may hybridize if the plants are allowed to flower and set seed, and their resulting seed and seedlings will have diluted flavours and scents. To prevent this clip and harvest the leaves regularly. This keeps the plants bushy and compact, and there will be no flowers.

Opposite: Harvest mint by nipping out the stems near the growing tips with your fingers or cutting them off with scissors. Regular nipping will prevent undesirable flowering.

Planting your mint medley

What you need
- multipurpose potting compost;
- horticultural grit;
- shallow container or trough such as this verdigris planter;
- 3 or 4 different mint plants (see p149) such as apple mint (*M. suaveolens*), pineapple mint (*M. s.* 'Variegata'), red mint (*M. x smithiana*), and Tashkent mint (*M. spicata* 'Tashkent');
- pots for potting on individual mint plants;
- decorative gravel for topdressing.

1 Mix the potting compost together with a little grit in a ratio of two parts compost to one part grit. Pot on all the mints into pots a size larger than the ones they originally came in. Water each well.

2 Half fill the planter with the potting compost mix, leaving enough room for the mints to sit on it in their pots, as well as space at the top to make it easy when watering.

3 Sit your mint pots on the compost in the planter. Make sure the tops of all the pots are level and fill in the gaps with more compost until it is up to the soil level in each mint pot. Water in well.

4 Topdress with gravel to keep moisture away from the crowns of the plants and to hold moisture in the soil. Water and feed the plants regularly to encourage growth.

Common or sweet basil (top right) is the popular choice for pesto and pasta sauces. Despite Greek basil (above left) having the smallest leaves of all it still has a strong flavour. Red basil (above right) has lovely, pungent purple leaves.

Basil

This popular supermarket herb is so much better when home-grown. Basil (*Ocimum basilicum*) is a perfect match in the kitchen as well as in the garden (see p27).

Basic needs
Sow seed directly into pots after the frosts, or into individual pots or modular trays indoors filled with multipurpose compost mixed with grit.

Growing techniques
■ Sow from late winter to mid-spring. Seed is light sensitive so press it gently into the potting compost and do not cover. Water well.

■ Seed germinates quicker on a warm, sunny windowsill, at 20–25°C (68–77°F). Once germinated set pots in a sunny, sheltered spot.

■ In cool-temperate areas grow basil under glass or indoors on a windowsill.

■ Basil hates to sit in water overnight, so water only in the morning; the plant can then use up the water before nightfall.

Problem solving
Spray plants with water or insecticidal soap if they are attacked by greenfly or whitefly (see p34).

Harvesting and storage
Pick young leaves regularly from the tips (see p155). Store in the refrigerator for a few days or freeze individual leaves, make into pesto, or infuse in oil or vinegar. Use the aromatic flowers in salads.

VARIETIES 'Cinnamon', 'Horapha', 'Napolitano', 'Nufar', 'Purple Ruffles', 'Sweet Genovase'

Oregano

Oregano (*Origanum vulgare*) is grown for its sweet, pungent leaves, which have a more intense flavour than those of its delicate sibling, marjoram. Some varieties make nice features in their own pot, while low-growing, creeping types such as 'Nanum' are perfect for edging larger pots. The beautiful, aromatic flowers attract butterflies.

Basic needs
Oregano needs a pot 30cm (12in) or more deep and rich loam-based compost or garden compost mixed with horticultural grit for drainage.

Growing techniques
■ Propagate from cuttings of young growth in spring, or buy young plants. Oregano does not grow readily from seed.

■ Plant in a sunny spot. Water well after planting and then regularly during dry weather.

■ Trim plants after flowering to stop them becoming straggly.

■ Cut down within 6cm (2¼in) of the soil before plants die back in winter. Mulch with grit to protect the crowns from winter wet. Protect plants from hard frosts with fleece.

Oregano leaves can be picked and used fresh, dried, or even frozen long after the plant has died down for winter.

Problem solving
Tends to be trouble-free.

Harvesting and storage
Pick bunches of leaves just before the flowers open and dry by hanging them somewhere warm, dry, and airy. Oregano leaves can also be infused in fragrant oils or vinegars.

VARIETIES 'Aureum', 'Compactum', 'Nanum'

Parsley

As it is one of the most versatile and common kitchen herbs, parsley (*Petroselinum crispum*) is an essential in windowboxes or in handy pots by the kitchen door. It is generally grown as an annual because plants go to seed in their second year and so lose their usefulness as a cutting herb. Choose from the many varieties of flat-leaved or curly-leaved parsley.

Basic needs
Grow in any container, including a hanging basket, with a depth of 20cm (8in) or more. Do not bother with the 'parsley pots' sold in garden

Curly-leaved parsley has a milder flavour than flat-leaved French parsley. For the best flavour add parsley just before the end of cooking.

centres. They are tricky to water and too small for parsley's large taproot. This herb is a hungry plant, so add garden compost or other organic matter to its potting compost.

Growing techniques
■ Sow outside in late spring, only just covering the seed with soil. Parsley is slow and sometimes erratic to germinate, although a warm spot, damp soil, and covering with a cloche will help.

■ Prefers damp shade so do not let plants dry out.

■ Nip out flowerheads to encourage further leaf growth during the growing season.

■ Cover plants with a cloche again in autumn to slow down winter die-back.

Problem solving
Slugs love young parsley plants so protect plants with grit or crushed shells (see p32).

Harvesting and storage
Pick fresh leaves whenever you need them. They can be frozen in sealed plastic bags or chopped and frozen in water in ice-cube trays.

VARIETIES curly-leaved: 'Champion Moss Curled'; flat-leaved: 'Italian Giant'

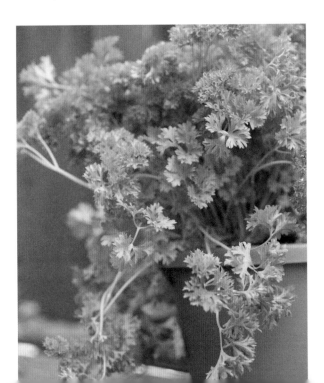

Taste of Italy

Italian food is all about top-quality ingredients and distinctive flavours and where better to get the best than from your own home-grown produce. This beautifully decorated, imitation-lead pot contains the classic Mediterranean ingredients of sweet peppers, spicy rocket, and peppery basil, bringing a taste of Italy to the garden as well as the plate.

Unless you start sowing seed very early in spring, it is best to buy young sweet pepper plants from the garden centre or by mail order since they need a long, hot summer in which to grow, flower, and ripen (see p83). This gives you the best chance of a crop. Basil seed can be sown from early spring onward and the timing is nowhere near as critical, but if time or space is short these can also be bought as young plants and planted out (see p152). The rocket can be sown all at once or a section at a time. It is very quick to bolt if conditions are not exactly right (see p135), and this way you can sow a section every couple of weeks and always have a new harvest coming up as another goes over.

Plant up this Mediterranean pot once all frosts have passed, sowing the rocket in the gaps in between the peppers and basil. Make sure the pot is in a sunny position to help warm and ripen the fruit. Pinching out the basil tips will encourage bushier growth and more young leaves to develop; it will also deter plants from bolting so soon. Feed the peppers with a liquid tomato fertilizer every week, once flowers appear.

Above: Most peppers will go from green to red and can be picked at whichever stage of ripening you prefer. Harvesting the first few peppers when they are still green will encourage more fruit, which can then be left to ripen further.

Left: Harvest young leaves of rocket regularly as cut-and-come-again salad leaves. Alternatively you could wait to harvest entire plants and re-sow for a new crop.

Planting your Italian pot

What you need

- imitation-lead pot, 60cm (24in) or more in diameter;
- drainage material (see p15);
- multipurpose potting compost;
- 2 x sweet pepper plants;
- 6–8 x basil plants;
- rocket seed;
- horticultural sand for sowing.

1 Line the base of the pot with drainage material and fill almost to the top with potting compost. Firm the compost down well with your fingers.

2 Set out the young plants, still in their pots, with the sweet peppers in the centre and the basil plants around the edge. Ensure each plant is evenly spaced and there is enough room for the rocket to be sown in-between them. When you are happy, plant and water in the peppers and basil.

3 As rocket seed is tiny it is helpful to mix it with sand before sowing, making it easier to see that you are sowing the seed evenly.

4 Scatter the seed and sand mixture across the surface of the compost and then cover it lightly with a sprinkling of compost. Water all the plants and seed in well. Feed and water plants regularly.

5 While the basil plants are still young pinch out the growing tips to promote bushy growth. Keep picking the leaves for healthy, compact plants. Harvest the basil (see p152), rocket (see p135), and peppers (see p83) as needed.

Rosemary

Rosemary (*Rosmarinus officinalis*) is one of the most useful culinary herbs, with a heady flavour that goes well with almost any food. It makes a striking centrepiece to a mixed herb pot, and its pale blue, sometimes white or pink flowers will attract bees to your garden.

Basic needs

Grow in a large pot, 20cm (8in) or more deep, filled with well-drained, gritty potting compost.

Growing techniques

■ Rosemary is more reliably grown from cuttings than seed. Take cuttings from new growth in spring and plant into seed compost. Alternatively buy and plant out young plants. Water well.

■ It favours a sunny, sheltered spot, although it copes with some shade. Young plants are vulnerable to low temperatures.

■ Pinch tips out regularly to keep plants bushy.

■ Feed and prune after flowering. Rosemary does not grow back from bare wood so do not cut it too hard; nor should you prune in autumn, when plants are vulnerable to frost.

■ Replace plants in pots every five years.

Problem solving

Rosemary beetle and its larvae feed on leaves. Shake plants and catch on paper laid below, then bin the paper and insects (see p35). Leafhoppers can cause mottling

You can pick the pungent leaves of this evergreen herb year-round for use in all sorts of dishes, from stews and roast meats to cordials and oils.

on leaves but this is mainly a cosmetic problem, as is froghoppers' distinctive froth on leaves.

Harvesting and storage

The leaves can be picked year-round but are a bit tougher in winter. Rosemary leaves dry well; they can also be frozen and infused in oils and vinegar.

VARIETIES 'Albiflorus', 'Majorca Pink', 'Miss Jessopp's Upright', 'Prostratus'

Sage

Sage (*Salvia officinalis*) comes from a large family of annuals, perennials, and biennials, all with strongly scented, sometimes coloured leaves and heads of colourful flowers.

Basic needs

Use a large pot, 20cm (8in) or more deep, with plenty of drainage holes. Sage needs very free-draining potting compost so mix in lots of grit.

Growing techniques

■ Grow from young plants for instant harvesting or sow seed in spring. Be prepared for a wait – sage is very slow to germinate.

■ Prefers a warm, sheltered, sunny spot, although sage tolerates some shade.

■ Keep plants compact and bushy by trimming stems regularly to tame sage's woody, straggly habit. Cut back plants in spring.

■ Protect less hardy, fruit-scented *S. elegans* in cool-temperate areas through winter.

■ Plants will last only a few years, especially in pots, so replace old, tired plants by taking cuttings of fresh, young tips.

Problem solving

Rosemary beetles and their larvae can be a problem feeding on the leaves and flowers. Pick them off by hand or shake them off onto paper; then bin it (see p35). Leafhoppers also cause a fine, yellow mottling on leaves, but this should

Common sage, with its distinctive soft, glaucous green leaves, is best kept compact in a pot by regular picking or trimming of the leaves.

be only cosmetic damage to sage.

Harvesting and storage

Pick the evergreen leaves all year round for use with meat, particularly pork. Sage is especially good with butternut squash. Leaves are best used when fresh because they are surprisingly difficult to dry well. However when dried the flavour is extra strong so use sparingly. Remove any developing flowers.

VARIETIES 'Purpurascens', 'Tricolor'; *S. lavandulifolia*

Thyme

Low-growing, fragrant thyme (*Thymus*) could not be simpler to grow, and once planted it can be almost ignored. Some of the prettier varieties of thyme, with their variegated or coloured leaves, are striking in mixed pots, particularly as edging plants or to fill in gaps, while the lovely flowers are adored by bees as they seek pollen.

Basic needs

Any pot, hanging basket, or windowbox with a minimum depth of 15cm (6in) is suitable. Fill it with well-drained potting compost.

Growing techniques

■ Buy young plants or split rooted clumps from established plants and grow them on.

There is a huge range of thymes and all are suitable for growing in pots, either as colourful edging plants or taking centre stage.

■ Plant in a warm, sunny spot, then water. Thereafter keep containers on the dry side; water only if there is an extended drought.

■ Pick leaves regularly to keep plants in shape.

■ Mulch pots with gravel every year to protect the crown of the plant from waterlogging.

■ Cover more tender varieties with fleece in winter to protect them from cold winds, frost, and winter wet, or move the pots to shelter.

Problem solving

Tends to be trouble-free.

Harvesting and storage

As long as you do not overharvest you can pick all year round. Thyme can be dried, frozen, or preserved in vinegar and oil. Its leaves make a great addition to stews, sauces, and marinades.

VARIETIES *T. citriodorus*, *T. pulegioides*, *T.* 'Silver Queen'

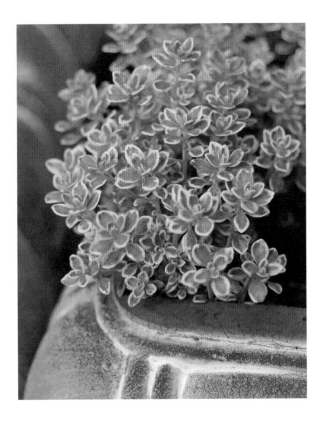

Herbal bath

A mixed herb pot, bursting with scent and an array of different foliage, is an attractive way to grow these useful plants, especially if they are complemented by a recycled container such as an old tin bath in soft, muted tones. You can enjoy fresh leaves whenever you want them – in salads, teas, even the bath – and at a fraction of the cost of the tiny bags available from the supermarket.

Most perennial herbs love a sunny spot and free-draining soil, so mix in plenty of grit or horticultural sand before planting. Feed plants regularly with a balanced liquid fertilizer, but do not be tempted to do it too often – if the leaves get too lush they lose flavour and aroma. Give the plants a trim in spring to encourage a new flush of leaves, and pick them regularly to keep them in shape. However you should never pick more than a third of the foliage at any one time, to keep plants growing strongly. To keep each plant's energies focused on leaf production deadhead the flowers, unless you wish to use them in salads.

Although the plants are all hardy, move the pot near the shelter of a warm wall over winter in cool-temperate areas and surround the planter in bubble wrap, making sure water can drain freely – the damp will kill the herbs, especially in cold weather. All these herbs need regular watering and feeding as well as repotting every three or four years, before they begin to get tired.

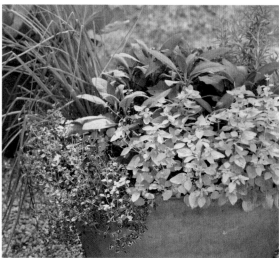

Above: Place the bath in a sunny, sheltered space out of cold winds and keep an eye on watering in very hot weather.

Left: Harvest leaves evenly from the tips of each plant to keep your herbs in good shape.

Planting your herbal bath

What you need

■ old tin bath; ■ drill; ■ duct tape; ■ bubble wrap; ■ grit; ■ loam-based potting compost; ■ herbs such as sage, chives, thyme, rosemary, and oregano (see pp140–157); ■ gravel.

1 Drill holes through duct tape in the base of the old tin bath – the duct tape stops the drill from slipping. Then line the sides with bubble wrap to protect it from extreme heat and cold. Add a layer of grit, to help water drain freely.

2 Add a mixture of equal parts potting compost and grit to help drainage further, filling the bath so that it is about two thirds full.

3 While they are still in their pots arrange the herbs in the bath until you are happy with the way they look together.

4 Remove the pot from each herb and plant them up, filling in with compost until they are all firmly in place. Water in well.

5 Topdress with gravel to keep moisture away from the crowns of the plants. Water and feed them regularly. Clip the herbs over regularly when they are in growth to keep them neat.

Edible Flowers

Allow a few self-sown borage plants to flourish around the garden to help attract pollinators each year.

Pot marigold flowers can be dried in a cooling oven and stored in jars for use long after summer has gone.

Warning: Some people have allergic reactions to unusual compounds in plants, so it is important to be cautious when trying flowers or unusual or new plants for the first time. The first time, taste only a small piece (don't swallow) and have someone with you. Wait at least an hour before trying more, and then take small amounts, tasting before swallowing. If it tastes bitter, too spicy, weird, or unpalatable, don't swallow it. Spit it out. An indication that the plant might cause a reaction is a swelling or other reaction in the mouth or on the lips on first tasting.

Borage

The vivid blue flowers of borage (*Borago officinalis*) are a long-favoured, edible delicacy. They have a cool, fresh, delicious, cucumber flavour, which enhances drinks and salads, and they freeze well in ice cubes. Bees and other pollinators also love these flowers (see p24). Try growing borage in a half-barrel with other such as pot marigolds (see below) and cornflowers (see opposite), or on their own, in a pot 20cm (8in) or more deep. Borage self-seeds freely.

Basic needs

Sow seed in spring and summer in a sunny spot. Borage germinates quickly, so you should be able to start picking within five weeks. Keep on picking to ensure your plants produce more.

Harvesting and storage

For flowers at their peak, harvest in the morning and use them fresh, dried, or frozen.

Pot marigold

The petals of pot marigold (*Calendula*) bring a bright orange zing and peppery spice to salads, rice, soups, and stews.

Basic needs

Easy-to-grow pot marigolds self-seed readily. They are happy in pots (see p164), as well as windowboxes, and are not fussy about potting compost or site, although you will get more flowers if you grow them in sun. Sow in spring and protect seedlings against slugs. Keep plants compact by pinching out their tips. Pick flowers regularly to ensure you have a constant supply. Wash off blackfly with insecticidal soap.

The charming, blue annual cornflower can be sown in autumn for larger, earlier flowering plants.

The beautiful heads of sunflowers follow the sun through the course of the day.

Harvesting and storage

Harvest flowers just as they are opening for use fresh or dried.

Cornflower

Curiously the electric blue flowers of cornflower (*Centaurea cyanus*) have little fragrance, yet they impart a sweet, spicy, clove flavour when eaten.

Basic needs

In an open, sunny spot sow seed in autumn or late spring in large pots filled with gritty, loam-based potting compost. Be patient – cornflowers can take up to three weeks to germinate. Keep the potting compost moist until plants establish, then slow watering down. Prevent the tall, wiry stems from flopping by discreetly wrapping bunches with thread, and prolong the flowering season by regularly harvesting and deadheading. The flowers are a target for butterflies and bees so dot the plants through your pots – 'Dwarf Blue Midget' is particularly successful used in this way.

Harvesting and storage

Pick flowers before they are fully open and use fresh or dried. Dry cornflowers promptly after harvesting by hanging them in a dark, airy place.

Sunflower

All floral parts of these vibrantly coloured plants are edible. Sunflower (*Helianthus*) petals have a slightly nutty taste, while the tender, green buds are eaten like artichoke hearts.

Basic needs

Sow seed outside from mid-spring into potting compost mixed with grit for extra drainage. Choose a warm, sunny spot. Cover pots with netting, and protect young plants from slugs and snails (see p32). Taller varieties may need staking.

Harvesting and storage

For buds, gather the flowers before they open. For petals, pick only the newest flowers (see p165), and for seed let the disc on the back of the flowerhead turn yellow, cut it off, and put in a paper bag. Leave until the disc is dark brown. Then eat the seeds or roast them to store in an airtight jar. Alternatively leave the seeds to ripen on the plant – they are much loved by wildlife.

Floral barrel

Edible flowers such as pot marigolds (*Calendula*) and nasturtiums (*Tropaeolum*) add a flamboyant touch to salads and other dishes, and they also look dazzling together in a large container. They are all easy to grow and will help to bring in pollinators such as bees and butterflies as well as beneficial insects such as ladybirds, lacewings, and hoverflies. Pot marigolds and nasturtiums may draw aphids away from beans, so nestle this pot among your other crops. The wooden half-barrel gives the whole planting a rustic air.

Grow your own annual flowers by sowing seed of pot marigolds (see p162), sunflowers (*Helianthus*) (see p163), and nasturtiums (see p167) early in spring and placing them on a warm windowsill until they are ready to go out into the half-barrel. Alternatively you can buy all these plants as plugs from garden centres or by mail order. As lavender (*Lavandula*, see p166) rarely comes true from seed, it is easier to buy pot-grown plants when your annuals are ready for their final pot. English lavender (for example, *L. angustifolia* or *L. x intermedia*) can cope better with wet compost over winter in colder climates than other French types (*L. stoechas*), which need lots of grit added to the potting compost for good drainage. The deeper purple-flowered varieties look best among the brightly coloured annuals in this combination.

Place the barrel in a sunny spot – good light and warmth will ensure lots of flowers and help to generate the essential oils that give lavender its beautiful fragrance. All these plants like free-draining soil, so add a generous layer of crocks to the bottom of the barrel before planting. Stake the sunflowers if they need it and pinch out the growing tips of the nasturtiums to strengthen the plants and encourage bushier growth. Once the annuals have all died back, cut back the flowering spikes on the lavender. Give it a further trim every year during early spring.

It is hard to believe that this striking pot is full of edible flowers, yet each of these plants will brighten a salad or add another dimension to a variety of meals.

Planting your floral barrel

What you need

- pot marigold, nasturtium, and sunflower seed, or young plants; ▪ small pots for growing on; ▪ half-barrel;
- drainage material (see p15);
- loam-based potting compost;
- 2 x English lavender such as *Lavandula angustifolia* 'Munstead'

1 Sow nasturtiums and pot marigolds in small pots of compost and keep them moist on a sunny windowsill. Thin out the seedlings once they have their true leaves. Pot on until they are large enough to go outside. Sow sunflowers individually in three pots and grow on the same way.

2 Line the base of the half-barrel with drainage material and then top up to about two-thirds full with potting compost, leaving enough room for planting and easy watering. Plant three sunflowers in the centre of the half-barrel, then position the nasturtiums so that they will cascade over the edge.

3 Plant the lavenders, and fill in-between with pot marigold plants. Firm the compost around the rootballs. Then water all the plants well. Throughout summer water regularly so the plants do not dry out. Give them a liquid tomato feed every two weeks.

4 Harvest the edible leaves and flowers of nasturtium regularly and pick the sunflower petals when the flowers open. Gather the pot marigolds and lavender when needed. Keep on harvesting or deadheading the flowers to encourage more to come.

5 Add colour and zing to a salad by sprinkling through some freshly picked nasturtium flowers and leaves. Both have a peppery taste similar to watercress and will liven up any summer meal.

Dwarf, clump-forming varieties of day lilies are perfect for growing in pots.

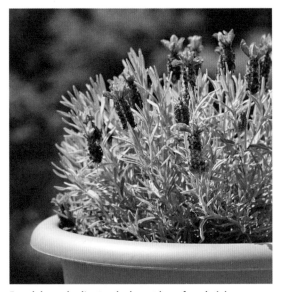

French lavender (*L. stoechas*) must have free-draining compost – that is its best winter protection.

Day lily

Day lilies (*Hemerocallis*) produce masses of flowers, each lasting only a single day, hence their common name. With regular picking they flower continuously all summer.

Basic needs

All parts of day lily, which are popular in Chinese food, are edible: the small buds can be eaten like beans; the unopened flowers are lovely in tempura; and the petals can be scattered on salads and soups. These tough perennials are easy to grow, doing best in a large pot or tub 20cm (8in) or more deep. Use loam-based potting compost for stability, since most plants are tall, or select dwarf varieties such as 'Cranberry Baby'. Plant in spring or autumn in full sun, although plants with darker flowers prefer some shade. For constant flowers keep the potting compost moist and deadhead as soon as flowers have gone over.

Harvesting and storage

Cut the whole plant down in late autumn and divide plants every three years to prevent them from becoming congested and pot-bound.

Lavender

Lavender (*Lavandula*) is a hugely popular flower, long used medicinally as a soother and relaxant, and it is now increasingly fashionable as an edible flower in biscuits, bread, or teas. There are hundreds of different types, and all look good in terra-cotta pots 20cm (8in) or more deep.

Basic needs

For the best flower scent plant lavender in a sunny spot (see p164), although it does tolerate some shade. Plant in spring or autumn in light, free-draining potting compost, then water. Do not overwater this Mediterranean plant, nor let it sit with wet feet, especially at night. Keep soil almost dry in colder months and protect plants against harsh winters. Give plants a close trim in spring, but do not cut back into old wood. Keep picking and deadheading flowers. Look out for rosemary beetle and its larvae, which feed on the leaves; shake them onto newspaper and destroy.

Harvesting and storage

Pick flowers just as they open and use fresh or hang up bunches for drying.

The much loved nasturtium is almost perfect in every way – beautiful, edible, and beneficial to the environment.

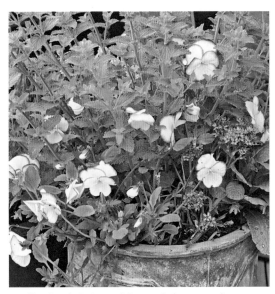

Deadhead and pinch out violas regularly to stop plants getting drawn and leggy.

Nasturtium

Another edible favourite is nasturtium (*Tropaeolum*). Its flowers, leaves, and even the seed pods are all eaten for their sweet, peppery taste. They are delicious in salads or when battered and fried, and each part of nasturtium tastes as lovely as it looks.

Basic needs

Nasturtiums thrive in containers, hanging baskets, or windowboxes filled with well-drained potting compost, so mix in plenty of grit. Sow seed as soon as temperatures are warm in spring (see p165) and keep plants well watered. Most will climb if you offer support, or crawl over the side of the pot if you do not. Nasturtiums are also useful companion plants (see p27), said to attract blackfly away from broad beans and cabbages, and encouraging hoverflies, which attack aphids.

Harvesting and storage

The flowers are good only when used fresh, so pick them just before eating. Harvest seed pods while they are still green. Gather the leaves when you want them for a peppery punch in a salad.

Viola

The much-loved viola has a sweet, fragrant flavour that is quite unlike the peppery punch of many other edible flowers. Violets (*Viola odorata*) have a pungent sweetness, while other types such as heartsease (*V. tricolor*) impart a lettuce- or pealike taste. Use the flowers in salads, desserts, and teas. In flower for a large part of the year violas also could not be easier or more rewarding to cultivate in your garden.

Basic needs

Buy plug plants, available from autumn onward; or sow in spring by simply pushing the seed into the potting compost. Leave the seed uncovered while it germinates. Violas are easy, unfussy plants and grow just about anywhere. They thrive in full sun, in any container, windowbox, or hanging basket 10cm (4in) or more deep. Keep deadheading plants for a continuous supply of flowers all through the growing season.

Harvesting and storage

Gather flowers from spring until early winter for use fresh, dried, or crystallized for later enjoyment.

Spring in your step

Sometimes you just cannot wait to get started because there is nothing more exciting than the first harvest of the year. This simple pot contains a selection of crops that can all be sown and harvested within a few short weeks in spring.

Speedy growers, which also make useful catch or intercrops (see p16), are ideal ingredients for their own dedicated windowbox. Start off the container in mid-spring, using light, free-draining potting compost and place it in a warm, sunny place. There is no need to feed these first crops because they are growing for such a short time and most compost has enough nutrients to last the few weeks that these plants are in growth. Water and weed them carefully, particularly in hot weather since spinach and lettuce will struggle to germinate if the weather is too warm and also bolt before you know it. Move the trough somewhere cool if the temperatures really heat up and keep harvesting the leaves, radishes, and spring onions when young. Pick and deadhead the viola flowers.

All of these crops could easily be sown continuously throughout the growing season for a constant supply. By switching to hardier varieties as the summer progresses this trough could take you right through to the following year. If you do extend the harvest, fork in a sprinkling of slow-release fertilizer when re-sowing, to give later crops extra nutrients. If the viola plants get tired, replace with fresh ones.

Above: This simple, pretty pot will keep you in edible viola flowers for fresh salads throughout the year. They should last a long time if picked over often enough.

Left: Harvest crops as and when they are ready. Pull the spring onions and radishes before they get too big and gather the spinach leaves and cut-and-come-again lettuce leaves whenever you need them.

Planting your spring pot

What you need

■ trough or windowbox, 45cm (18in) or more in length; ■ drainage material (see p15); ■ multipurpose potting compost; ■ 3 x viola plants; ■ sand for marking out; ■ lettuce, spinach, spring onion, and radish seed.

1 Line the bottom of the trough with drainage material and then cover with compost until the trough is three-quarters full. Evenly space the viola plants on the surface of the compost and then plant them, filling in with more compost. Water well.

2 Use sand to mark out where the vegetables are to go, sprinkling fine lines onto the surface of the compost. If you do not like the look of the design you can simply rub out the sand with your fingers and mark it out again.

3 When you are happy with the design for your trough, sow each vegetable seed into the sand. Then draw the surrounding compost over the seed until it is at the sowing depth recommended on the relevant seed packet. Water well.

4 Most of these seedlings should take only a week or so to germinate. When they are big enough to handle, thin them out carefully to give them room to grow. Remove any weeds since they will compete with the crops for water and nutrients.

5 Keep watering your trough. Radishes in particular can split if they do not grow steadily, and spinach bolts if conditions get too dry. Harvest the radishes when they are young and crisp, pulling them gently from the compost. Crop the other vegetables when needed.

Glossary

Annual A plant that completes its life cycle – germinating, flowering, and dying – in one year.

Bare-root A plant with no, or very little, soil on its roots when purchased.

Biennial A plant that completes its life cycle in two years.

Bolt/run to seed To produce seeds prematurely, usually after rapid flowering. Is generally caused by hot, dry, or sudden cold weather.

Catch crop Fast-growing plants that are sown and grown in the interval between harvesting a *maincrop* and sowing or planting another.

Cordon A *tree* or *shrub* trained as a single stem, and often supported against a wall with wires.

Cross-pollination/cross-fertilization The transfer of pollen from the stamens of one flower to the stigma of a flower on another plant.

Cultivar A contraction of cultivated *variety*, or cv. Refers to a plant that originated in cultivation rather than in the wild. Is often used interchangeably with the term *variety*.

Deadheading The removal of dead or fading flowers to prevent them from going to seed. This is done to promote further flowering, and to tidy up the plant.

Dibber A hand tool used to make sowing or planting holes.

Die-back [n] The death of a stem or other part of a plant after localized damage or infection. Often seen as discoloured patches on the stem and wilting leaves. Needs to be pruned out so symptoms do not spread.

Drill (as in seed drill) A straight, narrow, shallow trench or furrow in which seeds are sown.

Ericaceous Term describing any plant that needs acid soil (with a pH of 6.5 or less): for example, blueberries. Also refers to the type of acid compost that these plants need to grow in.

Espalier A *tree* or *shrub* with a vertical trunk and horizontal stems, often trained against a wall.

Fan A *tree* or *shrub* trained so that the branches radiate out in one plane from a single, short stem.

Garden compost Home-made organic material formed by spent plant material mixed with paper, cardboard, and some kitchen waste; this is left to break down into a humus-rich, dark compost. Is generally used for mulching and feeding the soil.

Genus A category in plant classification used to describe a group of closely related plants ranked between family and *species*.

Grow-bag A commercial plastic bag specifically filled with nutrient-enriched *potting compost* and used for growing crops, instead of planting them in a pot or the open ground.

Half-barrel A recycled container made from a wooden barrel that has been cut in half.

Heritage variety/heirloom variety Old, often rare, varieties that taste delicious or have an unusual colour or shape, and grow well on a garden scale. They are generally open-pollinated, which means they are non-hybrid and have never been genetically modified. Growers can therefore save their seed for use in future years.

Intercrop Fast-growing crops such as radishes that are sown between rows of other slower-maturing crops such as parsnips, thereby making maximum use of growing space. The intercrop is harvested before the slower crops are fully grown.

Loam-based compost A *potting compost* made from a mixture of loam, peat, and sand with added nutrients. It is best for large pots, since loam-based compost is heavy and stable, and suitable for thirsty plants, because it holds moisture well. Loam-based compost is often better for longer-term planting. Also called soil-based compost.

Maincrop (of vegetables) Those cultivars that produce crops during the main growing season. Maincrop potatoes are usually harvested from midsummer onward. They also take slightly longer than early-season ones to mature, and they are larger potatoes, taking up more room. They store well, unlike other potato types.

Manure Well-rotted organic material added to soil or *garden compost* to increase fertility. Is usually of animal origin.

Minarette A free-standing *cordon*, trained as a single, vertical stem.

Misting, hand Term describing the spraying of plants with a fine mist of water to increase the humidity in the air around them. Is often done to combat pests, such as red spider mite.

Mulch A layer of organic or inorganic material that sits on the surface of the soil or compost and reduces moisture loss, acts as a barrier against weeds and pests, prevents compaction, and helps to insulate plant roots against cold weather.

Multipurpose compost A *potting compost* made from peat, loam, sand, and bark plus some lime and fertilizers so it is suitable for sowing and growing a wide range of plants. Peat-free multipurpose composts are also available.

Perennial A plant that lives for more than two years.

Pot-bound Term describing a plant that has outgrown its pot and its roots have become restricted, causing the plant to grow poorly.

Potting compost A medium for growing plants. There are many different types including *multipurpose*, *loam-based*, *soilless*, and *ericaceous*. All include different constituents depending on the types of plants for which they are required.

Potting on Term describing the transplanting of seedlings or young plants into larger pots to give them room to keep growing.

Repotting Term describing the process of planting a container-grown plant into a new pot the same size, after reducing its rootball slightly to make room for some fresh *potting compost*.

Rootstock The lower section of a grafted plant, which controls the size the plant will grow to. It is joined to the *scion*.

Run to seed *see Bolt*.

Scion A shoot or bud that is cut from one plant to graft onto a *rootstock*. The scion is the upper section of the plant.

Seed drill *see Drill*.

Shrub A plant that has woody stems from or near the base but no central trunk.

Soilless compost A *potting compost*, usually based on peat rather than soil, but sometimes of coir or bark. Contains varying amounts of nutrients, depending on the use for the soilless compost: for example, seeds need fewer nutrients that longer-term plants. Is excellent for small pots, windowboxes, and baskets because of its light weight.

Species A category in plant classification used to describe a group of closely related plants ranked between a *genus* and *variety*. Such plants come *true* to type from seed.

Spur bearer A fruit *tree* that carries its fruit in clusters on short branches known as spurs. These take two years to form.

Standard/half-standard A *tree* or *shrub* grown with a single, clear stem up to 2m (6½ft). A half-standard is the same but shorter, being around 1.5m (5ft) tall.

Station sowing To sow individually or in groups of two or three seeds at fixed intervals in a pot or *drill*. This is a good way to sow economically and it reduces the need to thin later – just nip out the weakest seedling after germination.

Taproot The long, primary anchoring root of some plants that grows vertically downward: for example, on a parsnip or coriander plant.

Tip bearer A fruit *tree* that carries its fruit mainly on the ends of shoots produced the previous year.

Topdressing Term describing the application of a layer of fresh *potting compost* to the surface of a container to replenish nutrients; it is usually done after removing the top layer of old compost. Also refers to the decorative *mulch* applied to the soil surface around a plant.

Tree A plant with a central, woody trunk or stem.

True/true-breeding Term describing a plant that gives rise to offspring similar to the parent when self-pollinated; *species* plants come true from seed unlike F1 hybrids.

Variety A category in plant classification used to describe a group of closely related plants ranked below that of *species*. Is often used more familiarly and interchangeably with *cultivar*.

Index

Acknowledgments

The publishers would like to thank the following suppliers who have helped to make this book by generously supplying their products and time:

For cans, compost, fertilizer, nets and pots:

Julia Leakey at Crocus
www.crocus.co.uk;

Sophie Hedges at Garden Trading
www.gardentrading.co.uk;

Victoria Myhill at Harrod Horticultural
www.harrodhorticultural.com;

Andrew at Hen & Hammock
www.henandhammock.co.uk;

Emma De Maio at Stewarts
www.stewartcompany.co.uk;

Nicola Bacon at Westland Horticulture
www.gardenhealth.com and Marshalls Seeds
www.marshalls-seeds.co.uk;

Heather Gorringe and Sandra Montague at Wiggly Wigglers
www.wigglywigglers.co.uk.

For seed and young plants:

Janice at Jersey Plants Direct
www.jerseyplantsdirect.com.

David Turner at Mr Fothergill's
www.mr-fothergills.co.uk;

Sally Norman at Sarah Raven
www.sarahraven.com;

Francijn Suermondt and Shaun Brazendale at Suttons Seeds www.suttons.co.uk;

Julie Butler at Thompson & Morgan
www.thompson-morgan.com;

For helping us to photograph their pots:

Matthew Wilson, Victoria Kyme, Lucy Roberts and Charlotte Muswell at Clifton Nurseries www.clifton.co.uk; Mario De Pace at RHS Wisley www.rhs.org.uk; Jenny Richmond; Teresa Farnham; Don Mapp; Chris Achilleos at Marsh Lane Allotments; Mark Ridsill Smith; and Andy Male.

Photography credits

(t) top, (b) bottom, (l) left, (m) middle, (r) right

All photos by Steven Wooster except:

GAP Photos: 59 bm Zara Napier.

Garden World Images: 95 GWI/Flowerphotos/J. Buckley; 124 r J.Swithinbank.

Octopus Publishing Group: David Sarton 10–11, 14 tr, 123 b Gabriel Ash/RHS Chelsea Flower Show 2008; 24 l; 83 t; 130 l; 131. Torie Chugg 23 m; 42 t; 47; 48 l & r; 71 b; 71 tl. Stephen Robson (from Creative Vegetable Gardening) 68.

Suttons Seeds: 88 t; 118 b; 119; 123 t; 129 r; 157 t; 166 l.

The Garden Collection: 19 Liz Eddison/Design by Philippa Pearson/RHS Hampton Court; 25 tr Neil Sutherland; 35 t Bob Kennett-FLPA; 96 Derek St Romaine.

Thinkstock: Dorling Kindersley RF 20 t; 31 b; 70; 76 b; 100 l; 114 t; 134 l & r; 153 b. Goodshoot 74–75. Hemera 26 bl; 34 l; 42 b; 51; 69; 76 t; 85 br; 114 b; 160–161; 163 l; 166 r; 167 l. iStockphoto 8 r; 13 l; 14 tl & tr; 16; 18; 20 b; 23 t; 24 r; 26 br; 29 br; 30 l & r; 32; 34 r; 35 b; 40–41; 45 br; 46; 49; 50; 53; 61; 82; 92; 100 r; 101; 107 l & r; 108; 109 t & b; 112 b; 113; 118 t; 122; 128 t; 130 r; 135 t & b; 138–139; 140 t & b; 141 t; 142; 143 r; 148 b; 149 ml & bl; 153 t; 156; 157 b; 162 l; 163 r, 165 br.